How to Play Championship Tennis

How to Play

Championship Tennis

BY ROD LAVER

WITH JACK POLLARD

The Macmillan Company, New York

FOURTH PRINTING 1968

Foreword

BY DON BUDGE

The Grand Slam of the world's four major tennis champion-ships has been achieved only twice, and each time by a freckle-faced redhead. For twenty-four years I had the Grand Slam all to myself, and I got pretty attached to the honor, although I suppose I must have known, deep down, that it couldn't go on that way. One day a player would come along and equal my performance, even if he could never take it away from me or improve on it.

In 1956, Australia's Lew Hoad went close, winning the first three titles in the Slam—the Australian, French, and Wimbledon singles—but, when he got to Forest Hills for the fourth, his fellow countryman Ken Rosewall thwarted him. In the stand that day, watching Hoad's chance for the Slam slip away from him in a cold, swirling wind that upset Lew's serving power, was a 5 foot 9 inch 148-pound left-hander named Rodney George Laver. Six years later Rod turned out to be the man to repeat my Slam.

When I won the Australian, French, Wimbledon, and American singles in ten months of 1938, I didn't mention to a soul that I was gunning for all four. I figured it would only build up pressure for me if people knew what I had set out to do. It was only after I had won the Slam that the full heat of publicity was focused on it.

When Hoad failed and Laver made it, the Slam got the full treatment. Hoad and Laver probably thought about it as much as I did, but all the thousands of words that were written about whether they would make it must have worked on their nerves.

It is because I know this and appreciate how many years of concentrated effort go into fashioning the game which wins a Grand Slam that I have great pleasure in writing this foreword to Rod Laver's book.

As a tennis player, Laver can do everything, and he has exceptional control and versatility in his shotmaking repertoire. He only got that way after going through a very tough apprenticeship on the practice courts and in the tournament grind. In this book, he tells us about that tennis education, and tries to help all those who take up a tennis racket, whether for a social match at the local club or to try and match our Grand Slams.

Rod is not the kind of player who gloats over his victories, but the way he tackled the amateur tournament schedule and his intense application to winning since he became a professional stamp him with the mark of a great player. As an amateur he won every tournament every week on every type of surface, seldom having a lapse, and as a pro he has pitched into the Hoads and the Rosewalls. Every match is important to him. He is a good loser, but he hates to lose. That is the sign of a champion.

When I put together my Grand Slam, I had all kinds of aches and pains. In Australia before my final with John Bromwich I had to use a pencil and paper to talk with people because my voice had gone. In France I had stomach trouble, and at Wimbledon my voice went again. It was only the intensive training I had gone through before I started the hunt that enabled me to beat the abscessed tooth and the strain that caused these troubles.

Rodney George Laver had his troubles, too, on the way up, so the training methods he outlines in this book had to be right. Thus I have no hesitation in recommending it to all the millions across the world who play lawn tennis. Welcome to the club, Rod.

Contents

How to Play Championship Tennis

1. The Four Big Ones

My fingers couldn't seem to find any of my usual grips on the racket handle, and my mouth was suddenly very parched. The racket felt as if it were being tugged away from me by an invisible hand, and my leg muscles were on fire. I was out of control on the Forest Hills center court.

I had followed my serve in to volley at 30–all in the tenth game of the fourth set, and my fellow Australian Roy Emerson, suntanned leg muscles glistening from sweat, played a hurried, blocked return of service with his forehand. The ball looked an easy one to make a point on, and I was stunned when I volleyed it straight into the grass in front of my feet. My whole game seemed to have fallen apart.

Strain had never got me into its toils like this in any match I had ever played, but this day against Emerson, when I was only three points away from taking the Grand Slam—the world's four major national titles in one year—by winning the United States Singles, all the years of rugged training counted for nothing for a few moments. I took a couple of deep, puffed breaths, and moved uncertainly back behind the base line to serve again. I couldn't hear anything, and my body felt boneless. Somehow I got the ball into the air and swung at it.

I must have practiced that service swing so long it was automatic, because I managed to bang in three good serves. That was enough. Emerson drove two successive balls too long, and in the instant the second fell outside the base line I became the 1962 American Champion, 6–2, 6–4, 5–7, 6–4.

I don't remember going to the net to shake hands. I was just very sad knowing I had struck it lucky and that it was my friend Emmo whom I had had to beat. Then we were by the umpire's chair pulling on sweaters, and I couldn't pick up my rackets without dropping them, and all the world was shaking my hand. My sorrow for Emmo drained

1

away as I realized I had won, and I got this wonderful contented glow like a coal fire inside me, thrilled as I don't think I can ever be again. I had made it, I told myself; this was it—the Grand Slam, all four, the big four.

Don Budge, whose record I had just matched, was standing by the court exit, a little fleshy under the chin and around the middle at forty-six, and he must have been the first to congratulate me as we went off. The year Don won the Grand Slam was the year I was born, 1938. Only two of us had ever done it in the whole history of tennis. You could not have blamed him for feeling a little unhappy about my win. After all, he was the first. But he was very warm and friendly, a great sport, and I thought to myself that here was a champion in more ways than just a champion tennis player.

I had arrived at Forest Hills for the Nationals trying not to think too much about the Grand Slam, but as the tournament got closer I found the tension building up each day. All the papers had stories arguing about whether I could make it and comparing my wristy game with Budge's controlled power, and although I seldom suffer from nerves, this time it began to worry me. It was on the radio and on television, and I couldn't seem to get away from the thing.

A day or so before the tournament began, Don Budge invited me to go up to Grossinger's, the place in the Catskills where they train for heavyweight title fights. "It'll do you good to have an easy day away from Forest Hills," he said. We drove up in the morning, about one hundred miles, and Don and I had a match on the concrete courts there.

We made an interesting comparison. He was 6 feet 1 inch in long white pants, and he had lost the skinny look he had had when he was World Champion. His legs wouldn't carry him very fast, but when he got to the ball he still had wonderful control over it. I was 5 feet 9 inches in shorts, and as lean as Don had been in his prime. My game was based on spin, his on elegant, flatly hit shots.

We played a couple of sets, and, although Don was twenty-two years older than I, he won the second set. He still had that fabulous backhand, but of the two I'd say that Ken Rosewall's backhand is the best, because he gets such incredible accuracy with it.

When we came off the court Don said he thought I'd win the Grand Slam all right. "You've got every shot in the game, and there's nobody in this tournament to beat you. Get in and don't get too nervous. Play the game the way you can, and don't worry about the Slam." There was nothing in the papers about our workout, but I guess it would have made an unusual story, his helping me like that.

Looking at the draw before play began, I saw that I was due to play a string of rising players, any one of whom could really go mad on a given day. There was Frank Froehling, Antonio Palafox, and Rafael Osuna to beat before I got to the final against Emerson.

I was lucky to have Adrian Quist, the former Australian Davis Cup star, with me in New York during the tournament. Adrian, boss of the Dunlop sports goods firm for which I work in Australia, was in America on a combined business and holiday trip. He had come to watch Australia's boat *Gretel* make a great challenge for the America's Cup. He kept coaxing and advising me, and saying I shouldn't worry because nobody in the Nationals could do what I could with the ball. This steadied me down when the strain might have deprived me of the title. Budge watched all my matches and took me to dinner twice during the tournament. He is a jazz fan, and we went to places where I could forget about tennis listening to some wild music.

I went through to the final fairly easily, playing very nearly my best. Then there was just Emmo between me and the fourth title in the Slam.

Emmo was a little nervous, because he was the reigning American Champion, and I got off to a good start—unusual for me, as I am a notoriously slow starter. I had the edge through the first set after breaking his first service, which meant that I could concentrate on holding my own service. I took the set in eight games.

In the second set, Emmo was still a little tentative, and it followed the same pattern, quite good serve-and-volley tennis. I got the service break and served out the set. I could feel the tension growing all round me with every rally now, and I had the feeling the crowd favored Emerson. He was the underdog they wanted to see make a fight of it.

He responded to the encouragement and in the third set, after we had gone serve for serve, he finally broke through. Immediately I broke back on his errors. In the twelfth game of the set he got a passing shot that scraped the tape by me to get to 15–40 on my service. Then he hit one of the best backhand cross-court shots you could ever see to pass me as I closed on the net, and took the set.

I came out after the ten–minute rest determined to get a quick service break, and I got it in the very first game. But in the fifth game he took my service again to get to 2–3. I broke back for 4–2, and that should have clinched it. But every shot carried more strain until we got to that crazy tenth game. If you have never been through a few moments of torture like that you cannot understand how it is. Everything seems to seize up, your legs won't carry you where you want to go, your tongue feels lumpy. Only the drills I had learned twelve years before when I was ten years old had got me through it.

After the match Emerson and I had a beer or two together, and he was as happy for me as if he had won the title again. The celebrations went on into the morning. I was in a dream world far removed from reality for the next few days, and in no mood to concentrate much on the professional offers Tony Trabert and Jack Kramer made to me. I said I wanted to go home and defend the Davis Cup; they could talk to me then. In doing that I guess I was smart, because it jacked the price up a bit.

Only days after Emerson hit those two shots wide of the base line did I get a chance to reflect on my Grand Slam and how narrowly I had made it.

My bid for the Slam started in January, 1962, just before the first leg, the Australian Championships in Sydney. I decided I would try for the Slam with a fifth title, the glamorous Italian Singles, thrown in. After winning Wimbledon the year before, the Slam was the logical step forward, and by adding the Italian to it I would be after something not even Budge had done. Success in all five titles would boost the sum I would get for turning pro. The pros made such big money it was going to be foolish to turn it down, so I might as well get the best price I could.

I trained for about a month before the Australian titles. Sydney suited me, because the wind that invariably blows down the center court there helps my left-handed serve swing out of court. I dropped my first set of the tournament to Bob Hewitt in the semifinals, and was fortunate that Emerson came into the final worn out after two really arduous days.

Night matches for championship tennis had only just begun in Australia, and Emmo had had two days of hard tennis and two late nights of it on top of that. Only in the third set did he come near his best, and I went off to America a few days later with the first leg of the Slam in the bag by three sets to one.

I had some trouble with conjunctivitis in the United States Indoor Championship, where I lost to Chuck McKinley, but had got over it by the time I reached the Caribbean for the best series of tournaments on the so-called amateur schedule in tennis. They pay very good expenses down there, but you need the money because you go through some of the most expensive places in the world. It's a life of luxury clubs, sleek motorcars and beautiful suntanned women, swimming in the pools of luxury hotels and spearfishing at private beaches. The tennis was rich in variety:

Montego Bay on grass, Miami on clay, Barranquilla on clay, Caracas on cement, and San Juan on cement. Often it was so hot we didn't play until five in the afternoon, but sometimes even at 1 A.M. the courts still baked our feet.

I put a lot of my earnings on that tour into sideline fun, a working holiday on which I wanted to relax and tune up for the big matches later. At the Caribe Hilton in San Juan I played the roulette wheel where the night before a man had gone to bed winning $20,000. I went to bed having lost my appearance money from the San Juan tournament. That was the place where they refused to let Emerson and me go spearfishing because they said the barracuda were too vicious.

On we went to Italy, where I won the championship after Emerson had led me 2 sets to 1. This Rome event does not count in the Grand Slam, but it is just as tough to win as the Australian, and I can understand why some people want the Australian taken from the Grand Slam schedule and replaced by the Italian. The event is certainly more international in character, and with those zany crowds and on the loose, statue-lined Foro Italico clay courts that Mussolini built it's a really pleasing title to win.

Then on to Paris for the second leg—the French Singles at Stade Roland Garros, a very loose en-tous-cas court on the fringe of the Bois de Boulogne. Here anything can happen. You can't put the ball away, so most matches mean two or three hours in front of a noisy crowd, with unpredictable linesmen who speak a language you can't follow.

When we were down to the last sixteen players, I fell and chopped the top from my thumb while playing the Italian Jacobini. Blood poured from the thumb, and a bandage

The first of the four trophies in the Grand Slam, the Australian singles Cup. Laver surpassed even Don Budge's 1938 Grand Slam by also winning the Italian singles, a tougher event to win than the Australian title

wouldn't stop the flow, so I asked the umpire if we could stop while I had it dressed. He said no. We went on with blood running all over my racket. Jacobini knew I didn't want to smash and jar the thumb, so he kept throwing up high lobs. Somehow I got through in four sets.

Luck favored me again when John Fraser and I were eliminated from the Doubles, because this enabled me to get two days off to mend the thumb before I played Martin Mulligan, a chunky little Australian base-liner, in the quarterfinals.

In the fourth set Mulligan held match point against me when he led two sets to one and needed a point for the set at 6–4. My first serve hit the net, and I kicked my second to his backhand. He had been hitting them down the line, so I gambled and moved that way—and that is exactly where he hit it. I volleyed, with Martin scrambling desperately but failing to get to the ball.

Just after that escape I served a ball which Marty thought was a little long. I knocked the return for a winner, and Martin was so disgusted that my serve had been allowed that he threw a spare ball in the direction of the umpire. At that there was bedlam in the stands. Marty stood there in an argument with the umpire in languages neither could follow. After that he was too upset to play well. The crowd did not help him with their hoots, and I scraped out of it in five sets.

In the semifinals, Neale Fraser led me 4–3 with his service to come and 5–4 with his service to come in the fifth set. When he served leading 5–4 for some reason he stayed back, instead of following his service to the net. This enabled me to go in and hit the winners that got me out of another close one.

Emerson went crazy for the first two sets of the final, and I could do nothing to resist him. He played to my forehand instead of forcing everything to my backhand, and this surprised me so much I didn't get into the match until a crucial stage of the third set. We had a magnificent set, with the advantage seesawing this way and that, and again I just squeezed through.

In the fourth set, Emerson led 3–0, and seemed to have the title won when I hit a rolled top-spin backhand, a shot that had the crowd jumping for joy in those cold hard concrete stands. That gave me the big lift I needed. Emerson's reaction was to start playing safe instead of going for his shots as he had been doing. My temperament wouldn't allow me to do that. Whatever happened I was going to keep attacking the ball.

Afterwards Jean Borotra, Toto Brugnon, and the other experts said I had been devastating in the second half of the fourth set and all through the fifth, which I won 6–2, twice breaking Emerson's service.

With two of the four big titles won, I went to Wimbledon in fine trim, but a little nervous because of the added pressure of holding the title. The main trouble came in the quarterfinals against Manuel Santana, of Spain. He led 11–9 and 5–1, and had a point for a two-sets-to-love lead which I saved with a smash off the wood hit off the wrong foot. After this let-off I beat him in four sets, won the semifinal against Neale Fraser in straight sets, and retained the title by whipping Martin Mulligan; it was the second successive year I had won the final in under an hour.

My fifty-seven–minute defeat of Mulligan—the fastest since Hoad's defeat of Cooper in fifty-three minutes in 1957 —made me a strong tip for achieving the Grand Slam. But I knew from experience how your game could go awry in big tennis. My wins in Paris and at Wimbledon showed how much luck could influence a match. As it proved, I was right to be wary.

For those few moments of near panic against Emerson, all I had worked for seemed in jeopardy. Sound stroke-making was the basic reason for my success, that and sensible match strategy free of any nonsense, the way my brothers, my dad,

Charlie Hollis, Ian Ayre, Harry Hopman, Adrian Quist, and all the others who helped me had played it. There was no magic formula in my tennis, nothing every boy and girl could not copy. Sixteen years after I first took up a tennis racket I had mastered for a time the techniques that led to a Grand Slam and security for life as a professional. But my way to the Grand Slam was easy enough to follow . . . .

2. Taking Up a Racket

One night in Gladstone in Rockhampton, Australia, when I was ten years old, I sneaked out of bed and went down in the dark to the tennis court my dad had put down at the back of our house. It was nothing social, just one court and a little tin shed. There my elder brothers Trevor and Bob, and my dad—Roy Laver—were playing under lights with a tall lean man in well-pressed long white pants, named Charlie Hollis.

The court they were on was made of dirt taken from red anthills. You crush it up fine, spread it on clay, and roll it on with a heavy roller, and it's the best dirt surface in the world for a tennis court. I was mesmerized by the speed of Hollis's strokes, and I pressed my face against the wire fence enclosing the courts, concentrating all through the rallies. I had played a lot with Trevor and Bob and thought they were pretty good, but Hollis gave them a licking. His backhand was tremendous.

At the break after a set, Charlie Hollis went over to the tin shed and poured himself one of those rums they drink in tropical Queensland. "Bring that little kid out," he said, pointing to me out in the half-darkness. "Any boy as keen as that deserves to get a hit himself." My dad probably thought I should have been in bed, but he hauled me out onto the court. I was barefooted and in my pajamas, but it didn't worry Charlie, who started hitting balls back and forth to me.

Charlie studied my enormous freckles and my skinny legs, and, when we came off, my dad asked him how much he'd charge to coach Trevor and Bob. Charlie told him, and said, "Send the kid along, too. I'll coach him for nothing even if he is a midget in need of a good feed. He's got an eye like a hawk."

For every lesson from Charlie we got up at 5 A.M., and

rode our bikes about five miles to the Rockhampton Tennis Association courts, about one hundred yards from the hotel where Charlie lived. We'd try to get there well before the lesson started at 6:30 A.M., and my brothers would say I was the youngest and I should get the balls. Charlie kept them in a box under his bed, and I'd crawl in thinking he was asleep, and he'd hear me scratching about in the box for the balls. That way we would get half an hour's practice before Charlie got up. I'd hit the ball against a brick wall if there was nobody else around.

He would play with us until we went to Rockhampton Grammar School at 9 A.M. I've been all over the world and listened to all the great experts on the best ways of playing tennis, but I don't think any of them knew any more about the game than Charlie Hollis. He had been a well-known Australian amateur before he took to coaching, a striking figure—6 foot 2 inches tall—the type who takes pride in all he does, a man to stop the conversation when he enters a crowded room. The way he banged down that backhand of his, he was a real hero to us kids, and he'd argue with anybody about tennis.

Charlie had seen all the great players for forty years, and he knew from his own experience in tournaments how important a good, balanced temperament was to a tennis player. "I could get to the last sixteen of an Australian championship but no further because I'd blow my top," he would tell us. "I had the strokes to win everything in tennis, but I didn't have it in there . . . ," and he would tap his forehead.

My dad was a fanatical lover of tennis, and, like most people in the area, he would travel two hundred miles for a social game. He owned cattle properties most of his early married life, backwoods ranches where there wasn't much entertainment. We kids got most of our fun from trying to ride steers with only a surcingle on them. So Dad put down ant-bed courts. The last property he had, thirty miles west of Marlborough, ran about one thousand head of cattle, and this was where Trevor, Bob, and I started to play the game. Before we left the Marlborough property I went to the local school of about sixty pupils, and it was there, while he ran a butcher shop, that Dad first remembers my playing fairly sustained rallies. I won several school matches when I was eight years old.

Dad read every book on tennis he could find, and he used to hoard newspaper clippings on the game. When he moved the family to Rockhampton to give us an education, he would argue for hours with Charlie Hollis that my brother Trevor would be a champion. "Trevor's got beautiful strokes," Charlie would reply. "Better than Rodney's—but he's got an explosive temper like you, and with that he's never going to be a champion. Rodney's like his mother, quiet and determined. He'll make it, but Trevor won't."

The first thing Charlie taught was how to hold the racket, the right grips for each shot. He demonstrated the Continental and Western grips, but it was the Eastern or American grip he told us to use. There is no known grip, he said, which is ideal for every tennis shot, but, all round, the Eastern is the best of the three basic grips for playing tennis, even though you have to adapt it for some shots.

And so I have found it. I use the Eastern grip as the basis for all my shots, varying the position of my wrist slightly for some shots at the moment of impact. The wrist is the nerve center of every shot. Normally, I hit my forehand and backhand drives with top spin, hitting up from under the ball and rolling over it, but by resetting my wrist on the handle I can impart under spin or hit the ball flat. With a slight movement of the wrist, I can change a drive at the last moment into a lob, or hit the ball down the line instead of across court.

To find the *Eastern grip* you shake hands with the racket, spreading the index finger out along the handle like a trigger finger. The wrist is behind the racket. The "V" formed by the fingers and thumb runs straight down the

The Eastern forehand grip, with the index finger spread wide for added control

handle. Every shot in tennis should be played with the racket arm perfectly straight, never bent.

The *Continental* or *Hammer grip* was very popular after World War I and is ideal for low, slow surfaces and for

The Hammer grip, with the fingers all bunched tightly about the handle for a forehand. Exceptional strength is needed to use this grip success-fully

shots near the net. Pancho Gonzales and Earl Buchholz, fine players both, use it, but unless you have a wrist like a blacksmith—which, as Charlie said, few of us have—it is awkward for ground shots because the wrist is on top of the handle and not behind it. Fred Perry and Jack Crawford won world titles with the Continental grip, but today both teach the Eastern grip, and admit that if they were to learn the game again they would use the Eastern grip.

The *Western grip* is impractical for low balls, especially on the backhand side, because the wrist is on top of the handle and in front of it. Its one advantage is that it's easier to master the backhand, the shot that seems to give novices more trouble than any other, with the Western grip. On a surface like concrete which gives a high bounce you really have to work to beat a Western gripper because he can get so much top spin on the high ball, rolling right over the top of it. William Johnstone, Bill Tilden's old partner, was the last major player to use the Western grip for all shots.

"In the final analysis, the grip will make or break a tennis player," said Charlie. "We got to the Eastern grip after the Western and Continental grips had been found wanting. The English taught the Americans the game, and the Americans were smart enough to realize they could get more control with the wrist behind instead of on top of the handle. The first great player to use the Eastern grip was Tilden, and in a sense we are all his disciples. He could switch effortlessly from Eastern to Western to Continental grip for successive shots, but he settled for the Eastern grip."

Charlie went to great trouble to ensure that we understood the merits and weaknesses of each grip. "Now boys, what do you do if you meet a Western gripper?" he said. The answer we all learned: give the Western grip player low balls on the backhand because he cannot handle them.

The main advantage of the Eastern grip is the extra reach it gives you. Coaches never advocate any of the unorthodox two-handed grips, largely because they reduce the reach. The freaks and the two-handed players give the game color, but the average youngster would be hard pressed to get a single ball back by following them. The Italian Beppi Merlo, for instance, used a double-handed reverse backhand on the left side of his body, with his right hand further down the handle than the left. He hit the ball with the back of his front arm, if you follow me. For forehands he merely took the left hand off the handle and hit with his right hand halfway up the throat. But he had amazing control using a racket with onion-bag stringing and only about two feet of backswing. He was a real freak.

Since those early sessions with Charlie Hollis, I have always used the trick he learned from an old pro of putting hair oil on with my right hand although I am a natural lefthander. The reason is that Charlie wanted me to avoid errors through a slippery palm causing the racket to wander from the correct grips. He treated left-handers and right-handers exactly alike. There is therefore no reason for left-handers to approach tennis as if they were outcasts. Their technique in shotmaking is identical with right-handers, and they enjoy a few advantages over right-handers. I started school the first year they allowed natural left-handers to stay that way, and I've always been grateful my teachers didn't try to change me. Before then it had always been compulsory to write with the right hand. I am the only person in a family of six who is left-handed at tennis, but in games like golf or cricket, where two hands are used on the handles, I am right-handed.

Some players suffer a lot with sweaty palms and fingers. The grips on their racket handle become soaked, and you will often see them rubbing the handle on the net cord or on the umpire's chair to roughen the grip so that it won't slip in their hands. Sweat bands on the wrist prevent a lot of it by stopping perspiration from rolling down your racket arm onto the handle, but once you have taken the game on seriously you should give careful thought to what binding is best for you. Some players like grips made of leather with lots of punching, others use reverse grips. Adrian Quist always says I have a "grip phobia" because I always use new grips, never grips that are even a few matches old. I can take out the tacks that bind the grips to the handle, unwind, and replace the grip within three minutes. On occasions I have even made these repairs on court during a match.

Much of the trouble with slippery grips can be overcome by holding the racket firmly in the *top* hand when you are waiting to receive, with the fingers of your racket hand loosely enclosed on the grip. Wait for the ball with the racket held in both hands directly in front of your body. Keep your elbows out from the body to allow quick movement, and turn your toes in. The top hand does the work of thrusting the racket to the right or left for backhand or forehand, and it is only when the ball is very near that the racket-hand fingers move into position and become firm on the handle. In this way the throat of the racket (where the top hand grasps) takes a lot of the wear causing slippery grips.

Jack Crawford, the prewar World Champion who downed Ellsworth Vines, and my fellow Australian, Roy Emerson, both kept twisting the racket around in their hands as they waited to receive service. This wasn't a nervous twitch but their way of preventing both too tense a grip on the handle with the lower hand and the onset of perspiration. They don't know until the serve is hit which grip they will need, so they don't lose any time by using the twist.

To strengthen my wrists and fingers and to show me the importance of understanding my equipment, Charlie taught me restringing. I did a lot of it on and off for years. For beginners I recommend rackets that are not too tightly strung; with such a racket a child, for instance, will have more control of the ball and will not feel a shock every time the ball is hit as he would with board-tight strings. I started off with my mother's light flat-top racket.

The vital ready position, with the racket held loosely in the bottom hand, and the top hand ready to help thrust the racket into position quickly

It is essential, too, for beginners not to use rackets that are too heavy for them to swing easily. You don't have to use a heavy racket to hit the ball hard. I learned that in one of Charlie's first lessons when I tried the racket with which he sent down his big serves. Rackets that are too heavy are the main cause of sore arms and "tennis elbows."

Many parents send their children along for coaching with enormous rackets only a powerful man could wield comfortably. Then they wonder why the kids cannot rally for more than one or two shots. Pancho Gonzales always got plenty of power, but he used a racket weighing only 13½ ounces. Don Budge used a 16-ounce model without a leather grip. Among the top-class players I've met, that is exceptionally heavy.

The sports goods firms these days market good lightweight junior models ideal for beginners. I think grips about 4½ inches in circumference and a racket of about 13 ounces is right for the average youngster. Nylon stringing is a good idea, too, as it stands up to rain better than gut and saves money, since young people have a habit of leaving their rackets out of doors.

I enjoyed stringing my own rackets because, like most kids who are mad about a sport, I was very proud of my equipment. Even adults become very attached to their favorite rackets. I have had one or two in my life that were perfect, just a little light in the head and with exactly the right grips for me. With them I felt as if there was nothing there when I stroked the ball, but it is amazing how in a couple of years the glue and the paint in a racket dry out and change the weight. But to a small boy in a country town who has just joined a tennis club and is playing third grade, a racket of his own is a treasure. He guards it and sleeps with it under his pillow.

To strengthen our wrists Charlie Hollis gave us squash balls to keep in our pockets. We had to squeeze them whenever we thought of it. I squeezed that squash ball for hours on end while I was at school. It amused me to read in 1962 when I made the Grand Slam that "Laver's left arm is so strong it's ugly." Most tennis players end up with one arm bigger and stronger than the other.

"Laver's a little guy, but that left forearm and wrist— this is what he beats you with. That and his pride."

That is how amateur Gene Scott described my left arm for an article by American reporter Dave Anderson. "My racket wrist is maybe an inch thicker than the other," said Scott. "But Laver's left wrist is ridiculous. I'll bet it's two to three inches thicker. His whole arm is that way from the elbow down."

Scott and Anderson would have been intrigued to know that when I first went down from Rockhampton to live in Brisbane, five hundred odd miles south, and to concentrate on tennis as a career my left wrist was so weak I spent hours a day squeezing a steel spring in my left hand to strengthen it. Even my fingers have got muscles.

A lot of really good tennis players fuss too much over their equipment. They get to blame every bad shot, every loss on their gear. Everything from grips to racket weight, from string tensions to slippery shoes can be built into a mental problem.

Even the balls can drive some players crazy. In high altitudes like Mexico City or Salt Lake City, the air is so thin players can't breathe properly, and balls fly in a way they never do near sea level. It has been argued that one good method of bringing sustained rallies back into tennis would be to change the pressure inside the balls so they would not be put away so easily by the serve, volley, and smash specialists.

This knowledge of equipment is shrewdly taught by good coaches like Charlie Hollis and Dinny Pails. They also appreciate that you have to keep young pupils interested in the game, and they spice their instruction in tactics and stroke play with stories about great players and exciting incidents in Wimbledon finals and Challenge Rounds.

Charlie used to hold quizzes to keep his classes keen. "What size is a tennis court?" he would say, and if you couldn't answer "78 feet long and 27 feet wide," you would collect a penalty, for instance, hitting fifty serves. He told us stories of Budge and Ellsworth Vines and Fred Perry, and said he would give me Budge's backhand, Vines' service, and Adrian Quist's volleys and smashes. I became so familiar with the exploits of all the great players in the game that years later when I was on my first overseas tour I was introduced to Ellsworth Vines, and I said, "Oh, but I know you." No wonder Vines looked puzzled.

Although I was such a skinny kid, Charlie refused to put me into a gymnasium until I had been playing six years and was really hooked on the game. He did not want to risk *killing my keenness* with physical labor. Charlie and I would sit together watching tournaments, and when somebody fluffed a shot he would explain why it happened, adding "Never do that, Rodney," and I would answer, "No, Mr. Hollis."

To Charlie, parents were the worst enemies of good players he knew. He always fought with parents. Several times he almost came to blows with my dad through arguments about us Laver boys. Charlie reckoned I didn't have enough killer in me. Dad thought he meant that I was yellow, but what Charlie didn't like was that I wouldn't beat the other kids 6–0, 6–0.

Most of his early coaching was in the form of drills, and we only played a set or two to retain our enthusiasm. After two or three hours of instruction on the grips, you went on to the receiving stance and how to get into position for forehand or backhand, and then on to serving and the other phases of the game. We drilled until our muscles ached, and they went on aching long after we had stopped for the day.

We went through the drills for months, perfecting every stroke before we got to tactics. By the time I was eleven, I was showing enough promise for Charlie to take me with him when he went to coach the boys at St. Faith's Christian Brothers School in Yeppoon. He took me to build my confidence and give me experience but also to show the other pupils what could be done with an eleven-year-old.

Three nights a week he came to our house for dinner, and if I picked up the wrong knife or fork while we ate, Charlie, a very meticulous man, always immaculate, would say, "Rodney, if you are going to Wimbledon and Forest Hills you are going to need the good table manners your parents have taught you. Now pick up that knife the right way, not like a little savage."

3. Getting the Ball into Play

After Charlie Hollis had been teaching me for two years, there was not a decent bit of wire netting left on the fences of the association courts at Rockhampton. Charlie had us practicing serving into the fences for hours at a time, and the fences couldn't take it.

I would stand about six or eight feet back from the wire netting and serve at it. There was no net, nothing to aim at. The idea was to develop the correct toss-up of the ball and an easy, rhythmical service swing. Against the wire I could hit hundreds of serves; if I had been out on the court and had to chase the balls I would not have hit half as many.

I could serve when I was seven years old, but until I went to Charlie Hollis my technique was all wrong. My feet were too close together, and I lacked the easy Vines-type pendulum swing Charlie advocated.

The service starts with the toss-up, and far too many novices fail to give this part of the service enough attention. One by one Charlie took a class of about twenty pupils to a spot 2 or 3 inches behind the base line, 2 feet wide of the center mark, stood them body slightly side-on, toes about 18 inches apart forming a line pointing to the court at which the service was directed. Then he drilled them on the toss-up.

The idea is that you have to make the ball "sit" up there just in front of your head. If you hit it when it's going up or coming down it will seem heavier than when it's at the top of the rise. You "feed" it up in front of you. You don't throw it. The control comes from the fingertips, and when you hold the ball the distance between the fingers should be equal.

Watch Jack Kramer toss the ball up and you will notice that he pushes it up inside the hand, like a cardsharp palming an ace. The ball rises as if it is in a chute, and the basic toss-up routine doesn't vary, even if the position of the ball in relation to the head changes.

Charlie drew a half circle inside the court just in front of
where we stood to serve, and we rehearsed tossing the ball
up so that it fell in that area. Often you see boys and girls
just learning the game overbalance on the service swing, or
swing under the ball because they have tossed it too high.
Both are the results of failing to practice the toss-up.

Before you toss up the ball, check that you haven't edged
over the base line and are risking a foot fault. Hold the
racket in front, with the fingers of the hand holding the balls
supporting it. Take a look at where your opponent is standing, and decide then on what type of serve to give him and
where to place it.

Keep your front shoulder in line with the spot where you
intend the ball to land, body perpendicular. Spread the
fingers along the racket handle. I use a grip halfway between
the Eastern and Continental grips, but most good players
today use the Eastern grip on service.

The important factor is to develop a service which will not
unnecessarily tire you, a swing that is suited to your phy-
sique. I don't serve a very high percentage of aces because
I don't hit the ball hard enough. By getting my first serve in
I can keep my opponent back, but when I miss the first, he
can come in to attack the second. The effect is that I find
myself volleying *down* on the return of serve if my first goes
in, and volleying *up* if my second is returned.

Small men can serve with power if their timing is just
right, but it is generally the big fellows like Gonzales or
Barry MacKay who hit most of the cannonball serves. At
my height—5 feet 9 inches—I have to aim mainly at serving
deep into the corners, and at giving a variety of services that
will catch my opponents off-balance. One of my faults has
been my failure to smack my serves hard enough.

But at the start, don't try to hit the ball hard. Try instead
for accuracy and for a smooth service swing. Don't move
your feet. Start with the weight on the toes of the front foot
—the front heel should never touch the ground—and as you

begin the service backswing, take your weight back onto the rear leg. Keep your eye fixed on the ball, watching it right onto the strings.

The racket head travels up your back and over your shoulder as all the weight reaches the rear foot. At the moment the ball reaches the top of its rise the racket head should be as high up as you can possibly reach from a position perched on the ball of your front foot. The ball must be hit down into your opponent's court from the highest point of your raised racket.

Don't stop when you have made contact, but carry on the swing, following through and down across your body. You have not worried about the net since you steadied the racket with the hand holding the balls before the toss-up, but you have concentrated on where you intend to place the serve and the type of service it will be. And your eyes should not have left the ball for an instant.

"All the trouble in the serve comes from the toss-up or the failure to hit through the ball," said Charlie. "Girls particularly are inclined to pull up and stop the service swing once they have made contact, dollying the ball up like a lob instead of hammering down on it. Now, Rodney, let's see you practice the toss-up."

I took the ball and pushed it up with my arm stiff and straight as it reached the top of the toss. It was a good toss-up if it landed in the semicircle chalked on the court or if I caught it with my fingers in the same position above my head.

When I had done it several times to his satisfaction he asked me to stop. "Now, what height is the net?" he said.

*A useful trick in learning to throw up the
ball correctly. Paint in the area marked,
and if the ball falls inside it the throw-up
is a good one*

A   B

E   F

Lew Hoad serving (*Sydney Morning Herald*)

C
G

D
H

"Three feet at the center, three foot six at the top of the net posts."

You really appreciate the value of a well-drilled toss-up when you encounter a strong wind in a tournament on a fairly open field, for instance, at the White City courts in Sydney. The ball bobs about in the wind, and, unless you have the control to reduce the height of your toss-up, your serves will spray all over the place. I have seen Lew Hoad, who really likes to throw the ball up high, reduced to a state where he didn't want anything to do with the silly game because of what the wind did to his service.

One night when Charlie was at dinner at our house, we got into the usual heated discussion about tennis. "There are four vital qualities in a great player," said Charlie. "The first is a burning desire to excel, to be the champ; the second is a willingness to work for it; the third is to have the best technical knowledge—you can waste months on the wrong methods; and the fourth is a faith in yourself which is built up by a good coach. How do you think you stack up against all these things, Rodney?"

"Pretty crook, Mr. Hollis."

"You'll never make it using language like that. It looks as if I am going to have to teach you to talk as well as play tennis."

After I was equipped with the basic *flat service* swing— a swing in which you strike head-on into the ball without spin—we proceeded to the variations, the sliced service and the kick service or American Twist. Each stems from the position of the ball at the peak of the toss-up.

For the *sliced service* you throw the ball a little to the right of your head and in front of your body. You impart the slice by hitting across the left-hand of the ball as well as hitting down in the style of a flat service. The racket travels down and across the body, with your arm slightly bent. The slice is mainly used as a second service, because you have

Service toss-up. Left to right: kicker, flat, slice

to sacrifice speed for spin and accuracy. It is particularly effective on a damp court, which gives the spin more chance to work.

I have seen players highly skilled in returning service

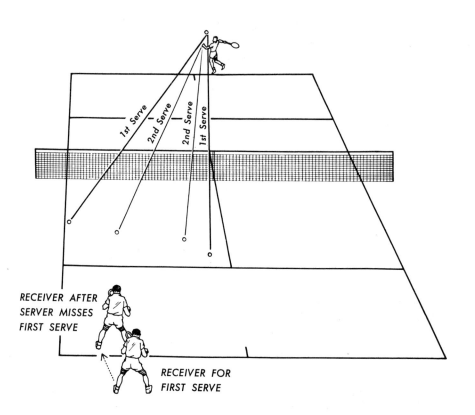

Service tactics. The first service is aimed at corners, lines; the second insures a correct serve

completely fooled by a well-disguised sliced service. They swung the racket to the forehand side and found the ball kicking unexpectedly to the backhand.

Charlie spent hours drumming into me that a left-hander like me gets far more natural spin and slice on his service. "Make use of it but make yourself the master of this natural spin—don't let it master you," he said.

To produce the *kick service* or *American Twist,* toss up the ball a little behind your head and arch your back as you swing the racket so that the strings move into the ball from the outside and toward the left of the ball. As the racket makes contact, you snap the wrist over and across the ball, following through down the same side of the body as your racket arm.

The kick service breaks the opposite way to the slice, swinging towards your opponent's backhand but often bouncing unexpectedly high. It comes off the court a lot slower than the sliced service, and this sometimes spoils your opponent's rhythm.

Neale Fraser, a left-hander, was one of the best exponents I have seen of cleverly mixed service. Neale could get tremendous spin on the ball when he was in his prime, probably more even than any of the professionals, and when he was serving well it was tremendously hard to break through his service.

Sports writers used to say that Fraser had a hoodoo over me. I doubt if that was true, although I certainly had a sort of hero worship for him because of what he could do with his serve.

"Fraser won Wimbledon, but Laver is the better player," Adrian Quist said in 1959. "Laver has a better backhand than Fraser, a better forehand, and a better volley. But Fraser has a better serve. That's why he won Wimbledon."

You get periods with all your shots when something goes wrong and you just can't seem to get them in or hit a winner with them. When that happens to your service, you are in trouble because it's the most important shot in the game. Hold your serve and nobody can beat you, even if you don't have another shot in your locker.

When I was almost twelve, I was serving well enough for Charlie to suggest to my father that I should enter the North Queensland Junior (Under Sixteen) Championship. Dad opposed the idea because he said the older boys would knock all the heart out of me. Charlie argued that I could win the Under Thirteen title so comfortably I wouldn't learn anything from it. It would be better for me to get in, take a hiding, and learn something.

My brother Robert beat me in the final after quite a good match that taught me plenty and stopped me getting too cocky about beating most of the juniors who came to play on Dad's court.

About that time I was chosen with another boy to represent Rockhampton Grammar School in a contest against Townsville that included all sports. When we got to Townsville, a hot, bustling port about thirty-five miles north of Rockhampton, the manager of our team was asked why he had brought the two little fellows. The answer was that we were Rockhampton's top doubles pair.

We didn't lose a set, and on the way back to Rockhampton I celebrated my birthday. But the celebrations must have got out of control a bit as I put my head through the carriage window when the glass was up.

4. The Hoodoo Shot

Charlie Hollis always taught the backhand before the fore-hand, the volley, the lob, or the smash because he said it was an easier shot to learn than any of these. Charlie, a keen student of young boys, saw that the sequence in which you progressed from stroke to stroke was important. He aimed to produce a master tennis player, but the parts had to be assembled in a certain order or the whole machine would fall apart.

He used to say that it was nonsense for beginners to be afraid of the backhand, as ninety per cent of ordinary play-ers were. In the beginning, both right-handers and left-handers have difficulties with the shot, and it often remains suspect long after all the other strokes have been mastered. Novices try to run round the ball to play it on the forehand rather than take it on the backhand, but to Charlie the fore-hand is a much harder stroke to control than the backhand.

"It is true that there has never been a left-hander with a really strong backhand," he said. "Norman Brookes, Jaroslav Drobny, Neale Fraser, and all the others failed to make their backhand reliable enough to withstand sustained pressure on it. None of them used it as a shot to hit outright winners. There has never been one left-hander in the whole history of the game whose backhand was not suspect. We're going to work and work and work and make you the first left-hander whose backhand is completely invulnerable to attack. Are you with me? Good."

At the start, my backhand didn't appeal to Charlie at all. The foundation on which he rebuilt my backhand began with the ready position he outlined in one of his first les-sons. Next came footwork, getting the opposite foot across the body and a little in front of it so that you turned side-ways on to the net. In my case, this meant thrusting my left foot across, but to right-handers it meant that the shot was

played off the right foot. "Why defend on the backhand when you can attack?" he said, and he would support this by hammering away a great backhand.

By the time the foot was across, knee bent, weight switched to this side, the top hand had pushed the racket down to the backhand side from the ready position and the fingers were starting to close on the handle in the backhand grip.

Today, to give more control, I use a backhand grip which is a quarter turn round the handle from the Eastern grip, about midway between the Eastern and the Continental grips. This places my palm on top of the handle of the racket instead of against its side. My wrist is not on top of the racket as it would be in the true Continental grip, but is slightly behind it. To brace the shot, I move the thumb up along the back of the racket: there is no question that this improves my control.

Charlie stood out in front of the class, with all of us in the ready position. At his call of "backhand," we would step to our backhand side, knees bent, and as we took the racket back we would slip the grip from the Eastern so that the thumb came up the back. The racket would swung back low down between our knees and the ground, with the racket arm rigid.

Then Charlie would walk down the class, checking each of our grips to make sure we had made the switch from the true Eastern grip. In two lessons the whole class mastered the change in grip. Nevertheless, any time our backhand missed, the first thing Charlie looked for was whether we had the right grip for the shot.

The crucial stage of the backhand after you have learned the right grip is the backswing. In fact, the backswing causes

Talented Australian Neale Fraser shows
perfect form as he hits a backhand (As-
sociated Press Photo)

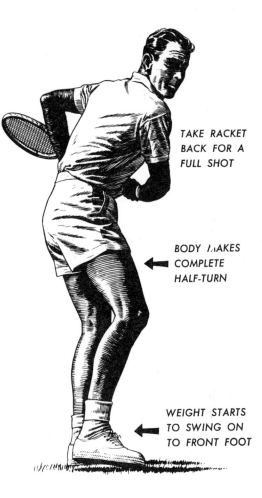

TAKE RACKET
BACK FOR A
FULL SHOT

BODY MAKES
COMPLETE
HALF-TURN

WEIGHT STARTS
TO SWING ON
TO FRONT FOOT

The backhand backswing

*Ken Rosewall reaches for a low back-
hand. He has not quite got to the ball,
but his wrist still controls the racket and
his concentration is well sustained*

more errors than any other factor. The backswing puts the racket on the various levels of the ball and also supplies the power. Take the racket back properly and you are well on the way to executing the shot fluently. But you cannot take the racket back at the correct level unless you have your feet in the correct position.

At the top of the backswing for the backhand, open the face of the racket so that you can take a full swing at the ball without discomfort. Don't try to block your backhand shots; hit them.

Immediately we reached the stage where we were ready to hit the ball, Charlie introduced us to spin, despite the fact that up to now we had not had lessons on the forehand, smash, lob, or volley. There are three basic ways of hitting a tennis ball: (a) flat, which is straight ahead with the racket-face; (b) top spin or over spin, which is hitting from under the ball, rolling the strings over the top on impact; and (c) back spin, which is achieved by chopping under the ball. Right from the start Charlie advocated top spin.

"Mugs hit over the ball; champions hit from under it," he said. "The secret of the champion is his command of spin."

Then he made sure all of the class was comfortably seated, and proceeded to explain how the ball bounces with the three types of spin. A flat shot bounces straight through. Top spin forces the ball to dip low over the net and keep low on impact, making your opponent hit up with his return. Back spin makes the ball lift after bouncing. The amount of spin you can get on the ball depends mostly on the strength of your wrist. Keep squeezing that squash ball!

Once we understood how the ball reacted to the three methods of applying the racket head to it, we were allowed to hit the ball with our first ground shot, taking the racket through to complete the backhand. We had to hit through the ball and not chip at it as many beginners do.

The wrist is bent for the backswing, but at the moment of impact the entire racket arm forms a straight line, with the

RACKET HEAD SWINGS UP UNDER BALL, ROLLING ACROSS TOPSIDE OF IT ON IMPACT

The rolled backhand

wrist tightly locked. Your weight is on the back foot for the backswing but shifts to the front foot as you strike the ball and follow through with a smooth, flowing swing.

Left-handers and most women tend to make contact with the ball with a slightly inclined (or tilted) racket face.

When we Laver boys were not on the court learning these things, we went swimming or fishing or kangaroo shooting with our dad or our uncle. I must admit I did not have much interest in school; all I lived for was the open-air life of sport and Charlie Hollis's coaching sessions. Spearfishing as a sport had just been discovered, and we boys used to go in off the reefs after the big fish that abound in that part of the Pacific.

The strange thing was that although we all loved the sun on our backs, we all suffered badly from sunburn because we were so fair-skinned. For years I tried all sorts of creams and lotions to try and protect my face while I was out on the court practicing. One or two of the creams were torture because you could not sweat inside them and your face baked inside the skin it formed. Finally I discovered a cream which enabled me to perspire freely without burning up, but even now every time I play in a strong sun I have to apply it carefully.

There were dozens of Lavers all over North Queensland, and they were all tireless, freckle-faced tennis fanatics. At weekends Dad and Mum and all the family would drive to friends' properties for a game, and I got used to people playing to my backhand every chance they got. A weak backhand is, of course, the first thing tennis players the world over look for in a strange opponent.

Dad was very pleased with the progress all the pupils in Charlie Hollis's Rockhampton tennis school were making, because he was the one who had instigated the formation of the school and had got Charlie appointed as coach. Before he came to Rockhampton, Charlie had coached all over northern New South Wales and at Theodore in northern Queensland, where he taught Mal Anderson. It must have been very satisfying for him years later when Mal and I were in the Australian Davis Cup team at the same time.

After he had taught me the basic backhand swing, the next step was to get me hitting a flat backhand, taking the racket head through the ball instead of chipping it. I had a little trouble for a while finding the grip with the thumb up the back, but because of his army-style drills I finally found it automatically whenever I switched to the backhand side.

"Now this is how Donald Budge played the backhand," he would say, and then demonstrate a lovely, smooth-flowing swing. He had studied Budge and all the other great players who visited Australia from grandstands in Sydney and Melbourne. Years later when I played against Budge his backhand was identical to the one Charlie had showed us.

I have always been described as a wristy tennis player,

probably because Charlie taught us top spin shots almost from the start. But as I am a comparatively short, wiry player I must have something to match the power of the big fellows. My spin does just this for me.

To give my backhand speed and power Charlie showed me how to take the ball on the rise—before it reached the top of its bounce—so that I could use some of the speed imparted to the ball by my opponent. I loved to experiment, to try new shots, even if this meant losing control of the ball.

Not to brag, I really enjoyed learning the variations of the backhand, whacking it across court or down the side line as Charlie called the shots. I had been playing to the very natural strategy of hitting the ball as far away from my opponent as possible, but now I started on something a little more subtle: tricking the character on the other side of the net to go the wrong way.

To smack a backhand down the line, you delay your swing and hit the ball just a fraction behind the hip. For cross-court shots, you hit the ball a trifle ahead of the front foot, hitting up from under the ball in a brushing motion if you want top spin. In competition, you often have to hit cross-court backhands as your opponent drives deep into the corner. You have to hit the ball on the run, and you have to hit it hard to make sure that you pass him and that he does not put away the volley he has followed in to the net to make. Don't let it worry you, though, because the cross-court shot is the most natural of the backhand shots. The down-the-line variety is hardest, because you have to let the ball get a little past you for it.

Some of those little fellows whose parents burden them with the leaden rackets I told you about find they can't swing the racket with one hand on the backhand side. This is why the old maestro John Bromwich and fellows like Pancho Segura took to the two-handed stroke. They got amazing control with it, but I don't recommend it for youngsters. Segura reckons he was such an undernourished, spindly

A   B

E   F

Sequence of Hoad playing a backhand (*Le-Roye Productions Ltd.,*
Beckenham, Kent, England)

C

D

G

H

kid he just had to use two fists to get the ball back. Never scold or punish a kid for using two hands; he is doing it from an instinctive desire to get more control over the racket. Instead, give him a lighter racket that he can swing with one hand.

When I was thirteen Charlie entered me in the Under-Fourteen State Championships at Brisbane. The week before the tournament started he sent me to Bundaberg to let me get my eye in and my strokes grooved in an under-nineteen tournament.

"Don't come back to Rockhampton without that State title, Rodney," he said, as I left for Brisbane. "Whoever beats you will be the winner."

"All right, Mr. Hollis."

Thanks to the warm-up at Bundaberg I was lucky enough to win the State Championship, and when I got home Charlie was the happiest man in town.

"How'd you play, Rodney?" he asked.

"My backhand was really bad, Mr. Hollis. It let me down. If the other kids hadn't been so bad I'd never have won."

"We'll start work on it first thing in the morning. We're going to get you the best backhand in the world."

That's how it was with Charles. No sooner had you learned a shot than you had to pull it apart and start all over again.

5. "Up, Change, Punch"

Just before my thirteenth birthday I played a very tall, middle-aged gentleman in the final of a Grade B tournament in Gladstone. After I had beaten him he went into the clubhouse, and said, "I didn't mind losing to a slip of a kid, but having to kneel down to shake hands with him was rough."

Charlie was moving me round from one tournament to another to make experience my teacher. I was pretty small, and that coupled with my age made me something of a prodigy in the district.

My parents kept a close watch on me to make sure I didn't get a swollen head, and I hope I didn't disappoint them. One experience that cut me down to size was when Charlie took me out to Mount Morgan, the gold-mine town, and made me practice with him there on the grass courts owned by Mr. and Mrs. Glen Shiels. It was the first time I had ever played on grass, and Charlie proceeded to further my education by chopping my game to pieces. He gave me undercut and he gave me slice, he dropshot me, he swung that big serve so far I was yards out of court trying to reach it. It made me appreciate that grass was different from crushed ant heaps or clay. I had to wait until I was fourteen to beat Charlie for the first time.

I began to have a little trouble with my volleys, and we had to go back to the beginning and fix it. We discovered that I was hitting the ball too late.

You should volley as far forward as possible. Go after the ball, don't wait for it. Rush into the net, and get the shot. Good volleying, as Charlie proved over and over, is ninety-five per cent confidence and five per cent know-how.

Keep your racket head above the wrist on impact, and never cut across the line of flight. On contact, the wrist is firm. The grips for your volleys should be the same as for the

WRIST FIRM
ON IMPACT

LITTLE
BACKSWING

WEIGHT ON
FRONT FOOT

The forehand volley

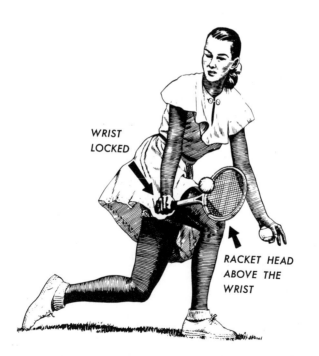

WRIST
LOCKED

RACKET HEAD
ABOVE THE
WRIST

The backhand volley

forehand and backhand drives, except on the high backhand volley. This is the only shot in tennis in which the thumb runs along the handle instead of clasping it.

Charlie used to teach volleying by breaking his class into pairs and instructing each pair to hit the ball back and forth across the net to each other fifty times without letting it bounce. He made a contest of it, and we kids were always trying to reach fifty volleys and then sixty and even better before the ball bounced.

"In tennis, you are called on to play just two types of volleys," said Charlie. "The volleys below the net are *defensive* volleys. Those above the net are *offensive* volleys. This means there are only four different ways of hitting a volley, high or low on the forehand and high or low on the backhand."

Our volleying drill was enacted on commands like, "Low forehand volley—down, up, down, up." At the word "down," the class would advance the front foot and bend low to the ground, feet wide apart, and at "up" we would make the short, clipped volleying stroke upwards with plenty of bevel on the racket. For the high backhand volley, the command was, "Up, change, punch." At "up" we got the racket into position, knees bent, feet wide apart; and at "change" we got our grip reset with the thumb along the handle. On "punch" we clipped the volley away. I got so that I could hear orders like "Up, change, punch," in my sleep.

Don't believe it when you hear people say the volley is a flat stroke, with the strings punching straight through the ball. Most of the best volleyers in tennis—players like Roy Emerson, Ken Rosewall, Lew Hoad, Margaret Smith, Mal Anderson and Frank Sedgman—all hit their volleys with a slight spin, the racket cutting under the ball on impact. This gives you control which is utterly impossible if you push the strings head-on into the ball. About the only time you hit a completely flat volley is when it comes to you well above the net and is a gift point you merely have to club away.

Laver stoops for a low forehand volley

The development of the serve-and-volley game in amateur tennis has seen a big general improvement in volleying standards. Since the majority of the amateur game's touring players work on the principle that the odds favor the net-

rusher more than the man who stays back and has to make
passing shots, we have a lot of players today who volley
well. One of the most reliable volleyers I've seen was the
American Budge Patty, who made his headquarters in Paris.

Former U.S. singles champion Mal Anderson demonstrates the drill for
a backhand volley

He used a very short backswing, and on contact pushed into the ball with the same wristy motion squash racket players use. He kept his eye intently on the ball, and as his backswing was so short he merely put the racket head on the ball, using the speed his rival had given it.

In the novice class of tennis, you can create mayhem by equipping yourself with a sound volley. For some reason a lot of beginners treat the forecourt like no-man's-land. They run away from the net as if they expect to get hurt standing in there. Get to the net first, and use your volley—even if it's the only shot you've got to go with your serve—and you put an awful lot of pressure on your opponent to pass you.

The key to good net play is agility, quick positioning of the feet, and fast reflexes, together with the familiar virtue of keeping your eyes on the ball and a vise-tight wrist on impact.

There is absolutely no danger near the net, and if you stay alert you can really enjoy the time you spend up there. The net protects more than half your body, anyway, and if you want to win, this is where you can swing it.

In the recent years of Australia's Davis Cup supremacy, there has been a lot of comment about Australian training methods. Many people have asked themselves how a nation of only ten million people has been able to produce, year after year, such a succession of champions. One of the eye-stoppers for people who come searching for an answer is our practice technique of putting one man on one side of the net and two or three on the other to hammer the ball at him. This is something Harry Hopman picked up on his world tours, and, of course, is designed to sharpen the volleys of the man who is standing alone behind the net. You can get pretty busy with three of your rivals plastering tennis balls at you.

A further strength of the Australian tennis structure has been the way the sports goods firms have subsidized the development of young players—one year to the extent of 100,000 Australian pounds! The promising players were found in district competitions playing for clubs whose officials recommended them to Slazengers, Dunlop, or Spalding. Executives from these firms would look at the newly discovered players, and if they agreed they had promise, the firm gave them a job with plenty of free time to practice or concession rates for their equipment. The year I won the Queensland Under Fifteen Championship, Charlie offered me to Slazengers, whose gear he always used, but they turned me down. The men who had a look at me for Slazengers decided I was too small to make the big time.

On the court nothing has played a bigger part in Australia's recent domination of world tennis than the superior fitness of its teams. But there is no secret formula in Australia's success, no magic, nothing up Harry Hopman's sleeve. It is just damned hard work and more hard work until your legs treat a five-mile run like a warm-up.

Volleying—the art of hitting the ball before it bounces—is the trademark of all Harry Hopman's teams. It is no secret that before the war when Australia seldom got to the Challenge Round, let alone to win the Davis Cup, our teams comprised good tennis players who usually clung to the base line. Since Australians have gone to the net to volley they have built a great record—which shows you the difference volleying can make.

I saw Frank Sedgman, the first of the modern string of Australian world champion players, hit some incredible volleys. He could volley winners from anywhere in the tennis court. Forecourt or base line, it was all the same to Frank when he was in his prime. He must rank as one of the greatest volleyers of all time, and, even now, when he only plays

Ken Rosewall hitting a low volley

seriously a few times a year, his volleys are tremendous. Sedgman in his heyday was so quick he could afford to wait and see what his opponents would do—anticipation was practically unnecessary.

"Grip the ground when you volley, for the love of Pete," Charlie would holler at me. "You're moving your feet like one of those wild horses you Lavers ride. Well, there'll be no buckjumping here. Start shuffling around like that and it's no wonder you hit them into the bottom of the net."

"Yes, Mr. Hollis."

"Who was known as Gentleman Jack? And why?"

"Jack Crawford, because he never said a bad word about anybody and always behaved himself on the court."

I remember once Charlie was watching Shirley Burton, the Junior Champion of Queensland, and Shirley missed several volleys. Charlie almost blew a fuse. "Four volleys in a row—and all of them winners! Gee, Rodney, I hope you never do that to a man. And all because she hit the ball too far back in the court. It was behind her when she started to whack it, instead of in front of her like this." He went through the motions of the correct volley, and to him it was the simplest thing in the world.

There is a school of thought among some of tennis's leading theorists—men like the former American Davis Cup captain, Billy Talbert—that you should never try to hit the first volley beyond your opponent's service line. The thinking behind this is that you are more inclined to error in the rush to get in to the net, and that by just getting to the net first you pressure the other fellow into putting up an easier shot from which you can volley a winner on the second volley.

I think it all hangs on whether you are hitting your volleys well or missing them. Confidence is the major asset in successful volleying, and my advice is that if you feel confident

Neale Fraser hitting a high volley

and you see an opening you should punch the volley into it whether it's the first volley or not. But if you have missed a few volleys and you are lacking confidence, then it is a good idea to set up the certainties with that first volley.

After the smash and the service ace, the volley is the most dramatic shot in tennis. You can play all kinds of tense singles, but crowds never seem to react as noisily as they do after a keen doubles volleying duel. The ball flies back and forth with each pair making three or four volleys, and it sends the spectators wild. The basic reason why Australians win all the big doubles events is because of their sound basic doubles tactics and their sharp volleying. You will never play good doubles unless you can pound home your volleys.

I would start hitting all my volleys in and making points with most of them and begin to be pretty pleased with myself. The thought would come to me that I must be hitting them the way Adrian Quist did, because Quist was the player we modeled our volleys on. Just to keep me from getting swollen-headed about it, Dad always took care to remind me that the pinnacle of achievement in tennis was to become an all-court player, not just somebody who could hit winning volleys.

At the Rockhampton clinic the class watched while I followed my serve in to knock off the volley. But it ended in the bottom of the net in front of me.

"What went wrong with that, Bobbie?"

"He didn't get in far enough."

"That's right—the ball was past him instead of in front of him, with the weight of the front foot behind it when he hit it. How can you punch the ball when it's past you?"

6. Do What the Word Says

By now my instinctive approach to match play was starting to show, and it was clear that I was never going to be a competitor who played safe. However far behind I was, I would always be a player who went for his shots and never tried to ladle the ball back like an elderly matron.

How could I be, when I cut my tennis teeth against two brothers who loved to belt the fluff off the ball, or tried to trick each other with placements and spin? My go-for-broke style meant that it would take me longer to control my game but in the end it would reward me more than by defensively patting the ball back and forth.

When Charlie Hollis gave me my instructions on the smash, and said, "Don't mess with the smash, Rodney—hit the bloody thing," it was the kind of talk I liked. "Doesn't matter if you hit them over the fence or into the next paddock or through a neighbor's window—do what the word says, smash it. The smash has to be killed, and you are only fooling with the game if you don't try to do just that."

It is best to add the smash to your stroke repertoire as soon as you have the volley licked. Actually, you should be able to smash as soon as you can serve, because the forehand smash and the service are played with precisely the same swings.

The only difference in the way I smash and in my serve is that when I smash I bring the racket up in front of my body instead of up my back. But the action of swinging at the ball from the backswing on to the follow-through is identical in both serve and smash.

Break your smash up into three spontaneous parts: (1) the racket goes up; (2) transfer your weight to the back foot; (3) throw your free hand up to balance the body. From that position it is comparatively simple to set yourself directly

under the ball and smash it with the swing you learned in
serving.

One of the secrets of how to hit a successful smash is to
take two or three little skips forward or back to bring the
ball down just a shade in front of your head. If you wait
until the ball is on you, you will find that it is either too far
in front or too far back to fall in the path of your racket. You

FREE ARM
CONTINUES
UP

FREE ARM
FULLY
EXTENDED

EYES HAVEN'T
LEFT BALL

RACKET
GOES BACK

FEET START
JUMP UP

do not have to be powerfully built to get power into a smash
if you get up off the ground to get it.

This is one of the shots I practiced a lot without a ball.
Charlie would call the spot on the court where an imaginary
ball would fall. From a starting mark several yards in front
of it, I would skip back, take off, to go through the smash
routine. I soon got the feel of the right pendulum swing, and

if there was not enough rhythm in it my instinct told me what was wrong.

"You learn tennis from the heart out," said an old tennis pro. For me the heart said "Attack the ball," and in no stroke could I do that better than in the smash.

You can work off a lot of steam in tennis by hammering away a smash. You fly up at the ball, and your irritation about line decisions, noisy spectators, or missed shots finds an outlet in the act of really clobbering the ball. I am fortunate that on the court I can usually keep my head, but I have seen some players get so angry that when they hit a smash they fired it back with a rich, satisfying glee. I have seen Australia's Bob Hewitt, who has a reputation for losing his temper, bring himself back to normal just from the pleasure he has extracted from one tremendous, successful smash.

Good smashing is not, however, all slather and blast. You certainly win points overhead by the speed of the shot, but constant practice hitting the shot with angle pays off just as well. By controlling the direction of your smash you can handle those really well-placed lobs that cannot be put away by mere power.

There are no contortions in a good smash. It is a fluent, coordinated stroke in which the racket head should always be in front of the hand at the moment of impact. When the hand gets in front of the head, your smash generally ends up in the crowd or in the net behind your rival's base line.

The grip for the smash should be either the Eastern or Continental, with the fingers well spread out on the racket handle. I use the same grip as I use playing the backhand— a quarter turn away from the Eastern grip. Ted Schroeder, star of several American Davis Cup teams who won Wimbledon at his first attempt, always used the Eastern forehand grip overhead. But it is a grip which I cannot recommend

Dennis Ralston hammers away a smash during a workout. If you can serve, you can smash for the swing, for each shot is the same (Ern McQuillan)

because you cannot snap the wrist down over the ball on contact.

To smash successfully, study your opponent's lobbing technique before you meet. Most players lob in a pattern. Some prefer high lobs, others use over spin, some hit lobs with a flat racket that imparts no spin, and a few hit them with back spin. But it is surprising how similar the trajectory of their lobs is from match to match.

By spending a few minutes familiarizing yourself with a strange opponent's lobs, you should be able to anticipate them when you meet him. This increases the time you have to make the smash, and you can be really demoralizing to him if, when he lobs for the first time, you blast it for a winner.

Frank Sedgman is perhaps the greatest exponent of the smash I have ever seen, although Gonzales has a mighty smash because of his great height. Sedgman's smashes always sound heavy, as if he somehow increased the racket's weight for just that shot. Lew Hoad is an expert at the smash, and when he is on his game that enormous right arm of his kills everything above the height of his chest.

I do not want to seem ungallant, but women seldom smash well, and many girls hardly ever play the shot. The reason is that girls usually suffer from the same fault—lack of mobility—and as a result they cannot move to lobs fast enough to get underneath them or if they do, are unable to get up off the ground.

When coaching young people I have often found them afraid to smash. They lack the proper confidence, because they are ignorant of the simple technique of how to play the shot. This applies to some really big names in tennis. More than once I have seen a highly competent player "freeze" on the racket as a lob approached.

Gardnar Mulloy, whom you would rate a really tough man on the court and never likely to suffer from tension, certainly did, playing doubles for America in a Davis Cup interzone final against Belgium. The Belgians soon realized that the aging Mulloy had lost his nerve on the smash and kept throwing lobs to him. It was sad to watch such an experienced player reduced to sending back soft returns on balls which, five years before, he would have pounded for the kill. John Bromwich won almost every honor in the game except a Wimbledon singles, but he was never a big point-winner overhead. Nor did Brom serve well, which proves the point that you only smash as well as you serve.

One of the basic tactical approaches to playing left-handers is to lob over their right shoulders when in trouble. A good left-handed player can overcome this by anticipation and swift footwork, just as a right-hander can dodge the lob put up over his left ear.

In fact, with good anticipation and speedy footwork, you can just about ensure that you only need a forehand smash and that the backhand smash does not have to be used. If you do have to play a backhand overhead, however, try to get the racket up in front of your body instead of round the back of your head.

At the hit-up before you play the first game of a match, always ask your opponent to put up a few lobs. This gives you a chance to get your smash swing working and to get focused on his lobs. Don't try to hit the smash too hard until you are properly warmed up or you may strain a shoulder muscle.

The ability to smash for long periods without missing one is the stamp of a first-class player. If your smash goes wrong, try to sweet-talk some confidence into yourself, and redouble your efforts to keep your eyes on the ball. Ask yourself if you are trying to do too much with the smash, seeking too much angle or spin. If the answer is that you are, then go back to the flat smash for a few games until you get your confidence back.

Hoad smashing

To ensure that the smash goes where you want it, line up the shoulder opposite your racket arm with the spot you are aiming at. Throw up that free hand, get off the ground, give it plenty of follow-through and wrist-snap, and you've got another point against your name.

I had been with Charlie Hollis about six years before I had a chance to show my smash to Harry Hopman. Hop was conducting a teenagers' coaching class for a Brisbane newspaper, and Dad asked Charlie to drive me the five hundred odd miles to Brisbane so that I could attend.

On the way south Charlie said, "Harry Hopman is a great man in this game. You cannot get to the top without him. You listen to every word he says and do exactly what he asks —but don't listen to anyone else except me."

In the dressing room at Milton, headquarters of the Queensland Lawn Tennis Association a few miles from the center of Brisbane, Charlie made straight for Hopman. He really gave me a great buildup, predicting that I would one day be Australian champion, and then running through what I could do with each of the shots.

"All right, then I'd better have a look at him," said Hop.

The story is that when Hopman came out of the dressing room for his first look at me, he saw leaning against the fence an undersized kid with a skinny frame, big freckles, and red hair.

"That him? Gee, he's little!"

"Wait until you see what he can do."

"Well, let's have a look."

We went on to a court, and Hopman said: "Okay, 'Rocket,' let's see you serve a couple." The nickname has stuck with me ever since, and when my game gets hot the headline

Laver leaps high to get on top of a smash near the net. The secret lies in positioning the body under the ball, in leaping off the court, and in a confident execution of the swing (D. D. & E. P. Schroeder, New York)

writers usually manage to work in something about the "Rocket." Originally, though, I got my tag the way "Muscles" Rosewall got his: the names suggested qualities we didn't have but surely needed.

"Serve to the corner," said Hopman, and I did.

"Serve down the line." I raised the chalk with one down the center line.

Now we went to the net, and it was bang, bang, bang with volleys back and forth between myself and the great man. At the end of the workout Hop walked over to Charlie, and said, "This kid's good all right. Got all the shots. Timing is good, and he's really quick around the court." Charlie beamed a mile wide.

I was in the class of twenty-four teenagers who went through the ten-day coaching course under Hopman. He impressed me because he really seemed deeply attentive to what he did. Everything he did himself had pep in it, and he never seemed to stop bounding here and bounding there.

One afternoon he had us hitting smashes at lobs he threw up himself, when Charlie wandered down to the court. "He's over-hitting these lobs," said Hop, as I banged a couple straight into the netting behind him. "Yes, but look how far off the ground he gets and the way he really attacks the smash. Rather a kid bang it and miss than be chickenhearted about it," said Charlie.

7. A Date with Marilyn

"I'll tell you about a bloke called Bromwich. I've seen him hit twenty-five ground shots to win a point. Not once did his concentration waver. He planned where he would put every shot well in advance of its execution. The length of his ground shots was so good not one of the twenty-five was more than two or three feet in from the base line. He'd put four in a row on a spot the size of a handkerchief."

We were going through the technique of playing the forehand drive which Charlie considered the most difficult in tennis, and he was hammering home to us the value of driving to a consistent length.

I seldom hit the forehand flat because I am a little fellow and I can't get right over the ball the way big men like Jack Kramer, Jack Crawford, Lew Hoad, and the other great forehand players have done. Charlie summed it up when he said, "Short blokes can't hit flat balls. Big men don't need spin, but the little runts like you do." You can get good length with the top spin I use, if not the pinpoint accuracy Bromwich got.

We would place tins on the court just in from the base line, and I'd try to hit them with forehand drives. I got so I could do it fairly often if I used top spin which made the ball dip down when it looked likely to go out over the base line. If I tried to do the same with flat forehands, the ball would invariably be too long.

A newcomer to tennis once watched the famous Australian Gerald Patterson spray forehands yards, time after time, over the base line. "He hits the ball well, but he seems to be accustomed to playing on a larger court," said the newcomer. You'd know what he meant if you saw me trying to hit nothing but flat drives.

Many things can go wrong with your forehand, but most of them concern the backswing. It's amazing how you can

Ken Rosewall demonstrating a flat forehand drive

suddenly develop a loopy backswing after months of taking
the racket head back in the right groove. The fundamental
slogan in producing a strong, fluid forehand from any position in the back of the court is: low ball, low backswing;
high ball, high backswing.

The forehand drive is often the first stroke people learn
to play well, but for years whenever people played Ken
Rosewall they always attacked on his forehand side. Under

pressure in the professional ranks Rosewall improved his forehand tremendously, but I would still rather go to the net on a ball hit to his forehand than on one aimed at that devastating backhand of his.

I have heard it argued that Rosewall had early trouble with his forehand because he was a natural left-hander, but how this reconciles with his great backhand I wouldn't know.

I was too young myself to see them, but wherever I have talked with people about tennis it seems to be conceded that the two greatest forehands belonged to Fred Perry and Bill Tilden. Tilden, it is said, got tremendous power into his forehands, Perry uncanny accuracy. The forehand drive was their main weapon in winning world championships. Jack Crawford always rates Perry's forehand the greatest the game has known; it must have been a really fantastic shot. Jack himself had a terrific forehand. I have heard good judges say they saw Harry Hopman running the wrong way again and again in matches against Crawford because he could not pick which way Crawford would hit his forehand.

Novices often make the mistake of playing the forehand facing the net. Instead, the shot should be hit with the body side-on to the net. You set up the shot by taking a step forward and across the body with the leg furthest from your racket arm. You now take your racket back with the forearm parallel to the ground as the weight swings onto the front foot. You move into the shot by thrusting your body forward, with the wrist relaxed until the moment of impact. Keep the racket head going as you strike the ball, taking it across the body in the follow-through. The worst mistakes you can make are to backpedal as you make the stroke, or take your eye off the ball. Stay in control, never indulge in unrestrained slogging. Rhythm, smoothness, and timing produce far more power than crude bashing.

The grip for the forehand is the basic Eastern, from wherever the shot is played. The time to hit it as soon as possible after it bounces without converting it into a half

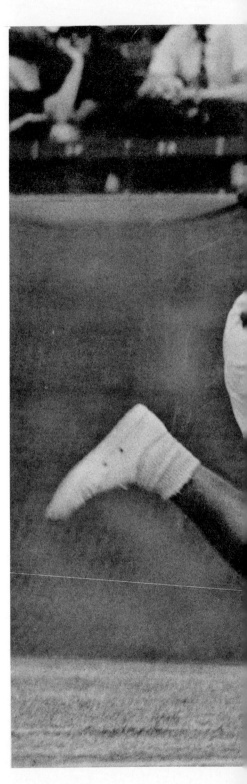

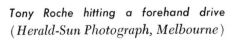
Tony Roche hitting a forehand drive
(*Herald-Sun Photograph, Melbourne*)

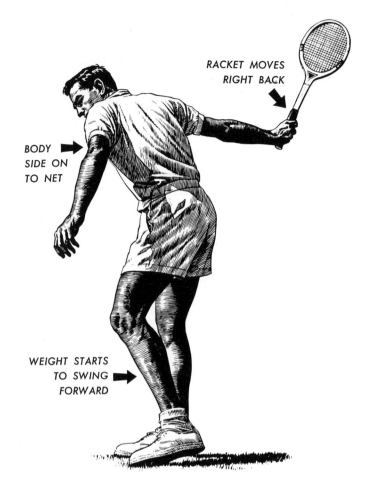

RACKET MOVES
RIGHT BACK

BODY
SIDE ON
TO NET

WEIGHT STARTS
TO SWING
FORWARD

The forehand backswing

volley. The place is on the forehand side of the body; never try to run round a backhand so you can take it on the forehand side.

Never hit a forehand off the back foot, always when you are moving into the ball. By hitting it while the ball is still on the rise after bouncing you gain a yard or so on the man at the other end of the court. You may get more forehands back by staying back and hitting them as the ball drops, but you will never be a champion unless you can hit them on the rise.

The forehand is the tennis shot most frequently used to set up winners, the shot on which most players go to the net. "A brilliant attacking forehand can be wasted if the player who made it did not move into position at the net to take advantage of the weak reply or defensive lob," Harry Hopman wrote in the newspaper during that coaching course.

We had gone home to Rockhampton after the course ended with mixed reactions. Hopman had confirmed Charlie's view that lack of the "killer" instinct was the flaw in my makeup. "He's too little," Hop had said. "He can't breathe with a sunken chest like that." This meant that if I really wanted to progress I would have to go into the gymnasium to try to cure or strengthen these physical shortcomings. Hop has always been a great believer in strong breathing as a cure

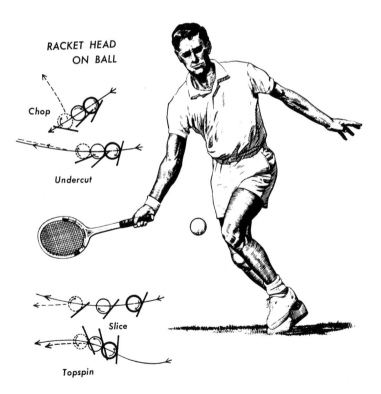

RACKET HEAD ON BALL

Chop

Undercut

Slice

Topspin

Forehand variety

for nervousness on the court, and even as a protection against cramps.

"Laver is a left-hander who is one of the best prospects for the Davis Cup we have in Australia," wrote Hopman in one of his coaching course reports. "I would not be surprised if he developed into the best player Queensland has ever produced. Of course, he is some years and a tremendous amount of work on his game and experiences away from that goal—but, fortunately, he knows it."

I was fifteen and about to sit for school examinations when I got yellow jaundice. I had to be isolated on a remote property run by a cousin. When I got well I didn't feel like repeating the year in order to pass the exams I'd missed. Reg Clemens, Queensland manager for Dunlop, came to town, and offered me a job in Brisbane, working with another promising tennis youngster, Frank Gorman, where I could get regular practice against a better caliber player than was available at home. Dunlop hired me as a messenger boy at £A4 17s. 6d. ($10.92) a week, and off I went to the south, happy to know that I was pursuing the only kind of life I cared about.

For a few weeks I was very lonely, and often after my day of delivering parcels for Dunlop was over, I would go to my room in the boardinghouse and work myself into a state of homesickness. Outside of tennis I knew no one in Brisbane. The letters from my family and Charlie Hollis's weekly messages meant the difference between staying and going home.

Frank Gorman was a friend of Jim Shepherd, another young tennis player; in fact he was dating Jim's sister, and we used to go to the Shepherds to play tennis. Eventually the Shepherds offered me a bed at their house. I moved in

Roy Emerson receiving. Note position of racket and wrist (United Press Photos)

with them, and it became a second home to me. Then from being a messenger I was transferred to restringing at Dunlop. I asked for it because I knew it would help strengthen my wrist. My brother Trevor had once completely restrung a racket in fourteen minutes, and I got pretty fast at it but not quite that slick. Several days a week I went to Snowy Hill's gymnasium to try and do something about my sunken chest. Snowy gave me a program of exercises to improve my shoulder and chest development. When I wasn't in the gym or out on the court practicing I was squeezing the squash ball in my pocket to toughen my fingers and wrist.

Now that I could no longer rely on Charlie Hollis, Ian Ayre—a former Davis Cup player who had been round the world a year or so earlier in an Australian touring team— became my practice-session workhorse. We played together a lot, and it benefited me tremendously because not only was he a keen student of stroke play and tactics but he could usually beat me. My strokes were well formed by now, but whenever I got into a bad habit Ian corrected me.

That year I won the Junior Championship of Queensland, and this got me a trip home to see my family. I look back over the years since then. Since I was fifteen I have always been away from home, never returning for more than a week at a time.

"Rodney, you are now on the bottom rung of the tennis ladder," Charlie said when he met me. "You are out of kindergarten. Only one thing can stop you winning Wimbledon—a swollen head. Knowing your dad and your brothers the way I do, I know that won't happen. Your next goal is the Australian Junior Championship and then the Australian Open Championships and finally Wimbledon. Win that and you will be able to say you can really play this game."

I was always very close to Frank Gorman, with whom I practiced regularly and who had been taken on at Dunlop with the same hope that in the next few years he would become a champion. Our friendship became one of the best things in my life. Playing tennis with Frank helped lift me from my normally shy state off the court and also vastly improved my game.

Frank and I would room together touring round the southern Queensland towns with Dunlop salesmen. We would give an exhibition and a coaching class for the local children, and then go round the local sport shops doing what we could do to drum up business. I loved these trips, and would wait eagerly all day Friday to get away on them. They gave me experience on all sorts of surfaces, downhill courts, bumpy courts, grass, and clay. They also took me out of Dunlop's Brisbane office where the time-clock routine irritated me.

Frank Gorman was a gifted tennis player. The experts said he was better than I was. He was a fun player, a character who could not resist trying something new on the court; he was always working out some new trick shot. He was also always in trouble for impetuous, spur-of-the-moment pranks, but people respected his independence.

We used to play sets for milk shakes or for a date with Marilyn Monroe for the winner. We always played better if there was a bet hanging on the outcome.

"It's match point in the Davis Cup Challenge Round, and you've got to win this point, Rocket, to win the Cup for Australia from the Yanks," said Frank, and we proceeded to play out a really exciting battle for the point.

Frank towered over me, for he was a big fellow, very handsome, and with a mop of wavy hair. Inside he was a very warm person, but he was brash as they come and one of the most self-assured people I have ever met. He probably could have handled the dates he won with Marilyn Monroe. I know I couldn't. I was too shy for that.

8. Lobbing for Laughs

Every lunch hour I rushed away from the Dunlop office to get in an hour's practice, and on two afternoons a week I was allowed to leave early for more of the same. I played with Frank Gorman or Ian Ayre, and when Harry Hopman came to Brisbane from his home in Melbourne, I generally had a game with him.

Frank became my doubles partner when we moved around to the country-town tournaments. We were very close friends, and nobody I've known has ever been able to get me to laugh and talk as freely as he did. I am normally very shy, but with Frank I could really open up.

I soon found that in our doubles matches the lob was a really valuable shot. I would even play it as a return of service to push the other pair back when they were right in on the net. After I had discovered how useful the lob could be in doubles I started to use it in singles.

The fun I got out of the game helped me tremendously. I really loved to play. Nothing would give me a bigger kick than to lure Frank in to the net and, when he was all set to volley away my return, to lob it over his head.

There are two basic lobs, the defensive lob and the attacking lob. The defensive lob should be hit high and deep to the far base line. You need it when you are caught out of position, and by throwing it as high as you can—about twenty-five or thirty feet above the net—you give yourself a chance to get back into position. You also give your opponent's nerves a chance to work in your favor while he waits for the ball to come down. The attacking job is frequently a clear winner. If it does not win the point it will at least tire the other fellow, who has to run back to retrieve it. This is a lob which has to be well-timed and concealed so that it surprises your opponent.

I could hit sliced and top spin lobs when I was only four-

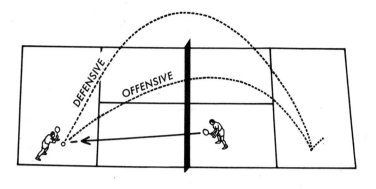

Lobbing

teen, thanks to Charlie Hollis's coaching. Charlie always says I am one of the few players who goes out and practices lobs. If that is true, it is because he convinced me that it was a vital part of my stroke repertoire.

Many young players consider the lob a shot for sissies and so seldom use it. This may come from their natural desire to smack the ball hard, or it may be because they have been watching girls play tennis and want to get away from all those shots that clear the net by five or six feet. But nobody can call himself a finished tennis player unless he can play the lob accurately, even in these days of power tennis.

By working on the lob I taught myself to hit it with the same swing as for a forehand or backhand drive. Running wide to a ball deep on the forehand, for example, I found I could roll the racket over the ball to produce a drive across court, down the base line, or a lob. The lob was almost always a winner because I learned to disguise it so well. For the lob I merely had to open the racket face a little more than for the drives, and this was enough to lift the ball over my opponent waiting at the net.

Most young players starting their competitive careers mistakenly believe tennis matches are won by hitting a stream of winners. They try to force the ball too much, and try for shots that are beyond them. The truth, often hard to accept, is that matches are won by the player who always gets the ball back, not by the player who hits spectacular winners but

Robyn Ebbern, top-ranking Australian junior of the 1962-63 summer, slides into a backhand volley, showing more confidence in the forecourt than most girls (Brisbane Telegraph Feature Service)

mixes them with errors. Hence the importance of the lob, the shot which enables you again and again to stay in the fight for a point, however impossible your position may appear. Never concede a point. When your opponent has you trapped yards wide of the court far beyond the base line, put up that high lob.

Readjust your thinking now if you consider the lob a defensive shot. It can be a very incisive weapon. Ken McGregor once confessed that he won an Australian Singles title by putting up a series of well-judged lobs. Frank Sedgman seemed likely to overwhelm McGregor by taking command of the net, but McGregor forced him back and finally rattled Sedgman with some delightful lobs just clear of Sedgman's head. Years ago Art Larsen won an American Singles by raising the base line chalk with a lob on the final point against Vic Seixas. Professional Bobbie Riggs, who won the last Wimbledon before the war, was notorious for the skill of his lobbing, and even great exponents of the smash like Jack Kramer frequently were routed by Rigg's astute lobs. Today Ken Rosewall's lobbing is achieving a similar reputation.

The grips for the lob are the same as for the drives. The place to lob is over the shoulder opposite your opponent's racket. As a left-hander I get used to lobs approaching me to my right. In fact, if you can keep the ball in court and put it far enough away from your opponent's free shoulder he will be compelled to run back to scoop the ball up, and this eventually will wear him down.

A few years ago the Austrian Ferdie Huber—the man they called the Danny Kaye of tennis—used a curious counter to this with which he achieved some amazing results. Forced to run back to a lob, Ferdie would play the ball back over his left shoulder with his back to the net. On the first occasion I encountered it, the shot frightened the life out of me.

The big secret in lobbing is to get under the ball. Your lobs will never be effective if you swing from the same level as the ball. Get beneath the ball as it approaches and aim for a spot about twenty-five feet above the net. Forget your opponent. Throw it as deep into the far end of the court as you feel is safe. The key is to guide the ball over the highest point your rival can reach, and this will vary according to the height and reach of your opponent. Obviously it is harder to lob a character like Italy's Orlando Sirola, who is 6 feet 7 inches tall than Ken Rosewall, who is 5 feet 6 inches.

At the New South Wales Championships in Sydney I played Vic Seixas in my first international match. Midway through the match he hit a good lob over me. Thinking he had hit a winner, I volleyed the spare ball in my hand at Vic, a prank many tennis players perpetrate occasionally. I was shocked when the Seixas lob was called out. The umpire gave the point to Seixas. Under the rules the umpire was right, of course, as I had caused a second ball to be introduced to the match while the other was in play. It taught me one of my biggest lessons. I have never played that prank since.

In doubles, the pair that commands the net usually wins, and one of the best methods of forcing your opponents back is to lob. Good doubles players are good on the lob.

Frank Gorman and I were always eager to fool each other on the court. A great guffaw would go up if one of us produced something which completely surprised the other fellow. A shot I learned in those happy days was when we suddenly found ourselves a few feet apart at the net. I would gently lift the ball over his head and wide of him, leaving him still looking for the ball to volley. Frank's face would crease into a big grin, and he would use his racket as a rifle and laughingly shoot me. He had great strokes and great vitality, but he was so highly strung he folded up from nervousness in serious competition.

I also found that, if a lob from Frank caught me by surprise, it was often better to give him another lob in return rather than try to blaze the ball past him as he came in to volley. When our touch was good, each of us could draw the other into the net with a drop shot and then drive him back with a lob.

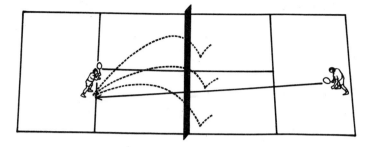

Drop shots

Start with the sliced lob. Unless other top spin shots come easily to you, stick with the slice. But whatever type of lob you play, try to surprise with it or it will not be successful. Shape to drive and, an instant before impact, slow the swing a trifle, open the racket face, and get under the ball. You control it with a flick of the wrist. The spin that the chopped action of the strings imparts will hold the ball up and prevent it flying out of court. Lob for the open spaces without trying to put the ball too close to the base line. Use all the vacant court available to you by lobbing across court whenever it is practical.

Frank and I always found when we went touring the country towns with the Dunlop salesmen that the lob was the most neglected shot of all among the school squads we coached. It was fascinating to show them how to play a lob and to pass through the town a day or so later and find how quickly they had mastered the shot. From then on the problem was to teach them to use the lob sparingly except when they were defending. About that time Charlie Hollis wrote to me asking if I would leave Dunlop for Slazengers, but I refused. He understood how I felt because Slazengers had refused to give me a job when they had first looked me over.

I won all the Queensland Age championships from ten up, but I missed out on the Under Seventeen—a character called Frank Gorman beat me in the final of that one. Frank probably had less trouble with my left-hander's game than the rest of the entries because he had played against me so often.

Charlie Hollis had overcome the traditional left-hander's weakness in my backhand by teaching me to hit the shot flat and with top spin, instead of slicing it as most left-handers do. Then I began to find out that the left-hander had some advantages of his own that more than compensated for having every player he met pummel his backhand.

"The advantage for a left-hander," Gardnar Mulloy once said, "is that he is used to playing right-handers, but the right-handers are not used to playing lefties. They are almost always playing right-handers, as there are very few in top-grade tennis. When you are playing a left-hander you have to make a big adjustment. The ball bounces in the exactly opposite direction on each shot. On a serve a left-hander's ball generally will curve towards a right-hander's backhand instead of his forehand. All the shots are that way. They bounce the other way than the way you're used to. It takes time to adjust to that, and by the time you adjust the match may be over."

On the tournament trail I had a fair share of success without becoming the boy wonder Lew Hoad or Ken Rosewall had been a year or two earlier. Often in junior events I found myself facing a black-haired, six-foot-tall youngster with very good ground strokes named Bob Mark.

I played for Queensland against Mark in the Linton Cup, a competition between Australian states limited to players under nineteen. With me in the 1955–1956 team were Max Collins, Frank Gorman, and Ken Fletcher. We followed a team that included Roy Emerson and Mal Anderson. The work of coaches like Charlie Hollis and Ian Ayre was beginning to pay off. Queensland, from being a Cinderella state, was developing into the most powerful in Australian tennis.

I was one of the pupils again at the annual Q.L.T.A. ten-day coaching class conducted by Harry Hopman in 1956. Hopman used me frequently as a model in this course, and often in my trips for tournaments or Linton Cup matches he put me through my paces. I was hitting the ball reasonably well, but I lacked Mark's reliable ground strokes, and he won the 1956 Australian junior title.

One afternoon at the end of the season I was on holiday with my family in Gladstone, where my brothers Trevor and Bob had gone into business in a sports store, when a reporter from one of the Brisbane papers rang up to tell me I was to go overseas with Harry Hopman and Bob Mark on a tour sponsored by Australian millionaire Arthur Drysdale. According to the reporter, the fares and expenses for the trip would cost Drysdale more than £A5,000 ($11,200). Drysdale, whom I had never met, had asked Hopman to pick the two juniors he considered had most promise.

I remember my reaction to the news—"Who? Me?"

9. The Ornaments

After the round of the Australian tournaments, a trip overseas is like a finishing course. With the finest guide of all, Harry Hopman, we went looking for experience for five months of that year of 1956, and we surely got it.

In Paris—our first stop on a tour which Hop had worked out with all the care of a hen brooding over her day-old chicks—I am reported to have said, "Gee, these courts are so slow you could sit down and eat one of those big French ice creams while you wait for the ball to come back." I meant it, too. I simply could not believe a tennis court could be so slow. It was as if they had thrown the clay down to make a court and forgotten to roll it or bind it in any way. Every time the ball bounced it left a six- to eight-inch mark on the court.

I was desperately keen to do well, and in my anxiety to make the folks back home proud of me I hit myself right out of the tournament, going for every shot as if I intended to carve the cover from the ball. Somebody whose name I cannot pronounce and who has not been heard of since put me out of the tournament in straight sets.

For hours every day, though, Mark and I went down to a back court, and there it was bang, bang with Hop putting in a word here, chasing a ball for us there, coaxing, encouraging. The matches were soon over for us, but while the crowds were all in on the main court watching the titles decided we were down on a back court, with Hop saying, "Not bad, but try it again with a little more this or that."

I had never met anybody with "duke" or "earl" to his name, but I met a few when we went to Wimbledon. The grass there was far more to my liking. I could get speed, and I liked that. Wimbledon, in fact, has the fastest grass courts in the world, with hardly a bump or an uneven patch on any of them. The whole setup was a revelation, from the big black limousines with the All-England Club pennants out front that called to take us to and from the courts, to that wonderful center court enclosed by ivy-draped stands. Hop, of course, had been there often before; he knew everybody, and he made sure we were shown the right way to do everything.

Little things nobody else worries about or even thinks about help to make Wimbledon. The balls on the center court, for instance, are kept in special refrigerated boxes behind the umpire's chair to make sure they will bounce properly. The ballboys are put through a course in fielding before the tournament starts, so that when they dash across the court at a tense moment in a match they will pick up the ball on the first grab and not hold everyone up while they scramble for it. One year Jaroslav Drobny and Budge Patty played the longest match in Wimbledon history—ninety-three games altogether—and the very next morning they got an invitation to lunch with the All-England Club committee. At the lunch they were presented with cigarette cases commemorating their match, with the scores of the match that had finish at nine o'clock the night before engraved on them.

In the face of all of this, I was just a shy, open-mouthed kid, I guess, but I was happy. I think I won one or two matches in the open singles before I was eliminated, and Mark and I did fairly well in getting to the last sixteen in doubles. I was mainly concerned with the junior singles event, the so-called Junior World Championships, to which one junior is nominated by each country. I was runner-up to Ron Holmberg, a performance I was very pleased about, because Ron had been on the previous year's American Davis Cup team.

On a tour like that a newcomer learns a lot about the rule book. I was typical of most young Australians: I had put most of my effort into learning the strokes and not enough into the rules which governed the use of those shots.

For example, I was intrigued to see how quickly overseas

umpires called "foul shot" when a ball was struck twice or touched part of a player's clothes. I had always been a little vague about the rule on rackets clashing in doubles. On this tour I found in matches with Mark that the rule clearly set out that only one racket could stroke the ball although the other racket could come up from behind it and supply extra impetus. If both rackets touched the ball it was a foul shot.

Wimbledon, I discovered, is the toughest test of all for a player's physical resources, for this is the only major event in which there is no break after the third set. The conditions of the tournament say, "Play shall be continuous"—and it is. This meant that if we were doing something wrong we had to work out the answers ourselves. There was no ten-minute spell in which Hop could give us the answers.

Playing on the Continent after Wimbledon I heard quite a lot of talk among regulars on the European amateur circuit about stalling. Most of the boys gave the Oscar to Budge Patty, with Merv Rose pressing him hard. These were the champions in the gentle art of getting your breath back while you fumbled with the balls or asked a ballboy to move or stand still.

On very soft clay courts where the ball leaves a mark as big as a footprint, I found that it was common for puffs of chalk to rise as a ball landed and for the shot to be called out. The reason was that the chalk lifts from the lines and is spread outside the line. A bigger problem to a visiting player, however, is the language barrier. I could play several rallies without having a clue as to what the score was.

Big Ken McGregor, who partnered Sedgman in some great Davis Cup wins, was playing a match in Paris one year when along came Tony Trabert. "What's the score, Macca?" said Trabert.

"Don't know," said McGregor, "but I think it's a set all and I'm leading in the third."

Trabert, who could speak a little French, walked to the

umpire's chair and back quickly to tell McGregor, "Say, Macca, you better get going. It's two sets to love against you and you're trailing 0–2 in the third."

You encounter such a variety of surfaces when you travel from country to country as we did that you cannot fail to improve your knowledge of what Charlie Hollis calls the ornaments of the game: chop, spin, dinks, stop volleys, drop shots, half volleys, fading the ball across an opponent's body, and the smash you play at a high bounding ball that has bounced on your own side of the net.

For full-length drives directed towards your opponent's base line, steer clear of chop. Its main use is in dinks: short-length cross-court shots played from below net level, racket head above the wrist, little pushes that can break up your opponent's stroking rhythm and get him running wide so that he leaves the court open in returning the ball. Ken Rosewall can play a terrific faded shot when you serve wide to his backhand side. He has developed such phenomenal accuracy with it, he can land it on a bank note. Without opening the face of the racket, he slows down the swing and drifts the ball just over the net to your backhand. It means that you have to dig his return up from your toes, and you have to be quick to get in there or on some surfaces it will bounce a second time before you arrive.

Dinks are particularly useful in doubles when you can angle the short shots a lot more than in singles, but you must bend the knees for them. You can pick up a shot on one side of the court and push it over the net to the opposite side and make your opponents run back for it.

Chop causes a big loss of accuracy, and is the action of chopping the racket head down with a hatchet-like swing onto and under the ball. The racket head starts above the level of the ball. Slice is imparted by swinging down under the ball at the end of an open-faced swing.

Chop balloons the ball a little as it passes over the net, and is hard to control. Slice can be controlled more, and is really useful in slowing down the game of an opponent who likes plenty of speed.

I like to hit a sliced or flatly hit shot on which to go to the net. The ball keeps low, and your opponent cannot hit it as strongly as a flat shot. The great value of top spin is in upsetting a net-rusher. Using top spin you can aim higher above the net than for a flatly hit shot, because you know the top spin will bring it down. The volleyer has to bend low to get top spin back and must hit up as the ball dips after passing the net.

One of the most effective uses of chop and slice is on the return of service. By adopting the alert ready position you can take all the power from your rival's service with a well-played chop, and you can get reasonable length on it. It is very handy for countering a high kicking service.

Now and then you get a ball which bounces so high you cannot play your normal ground shots but which does not get up high enough to smash. This is a good time to employ chop or slice.

Never attempt to vary the pace of a match unless you are sure you can handle the switch from your basic game to spin shots and back again. But there are few better methods of probing for weaknesses in the opposition than by mixing up flatly hit and top spin shots with a little slice or chop. Vary the shots from one stroke to another. Don't play one entire rally with chop and then all the next with flatly hit shots.

The stop volley is hit with back spin, and its effect is to make the ball hug the ground once it bounces. At the moment of impact you loosen the wrist slightly and give the ball just a fraction of chop. Don't follow through and the ball will just lie on the court with barely any bounce.

Laver turns the racket head in preparation for a deft, sliced drop shot. Shots like this should only be attempted when the ball is above net high (Trenoweth-Colorcraft Photography, North Sydney)

Ralston scrambles back a half volley on the backhand wing. The half volley should only be played when no other shot is possible, for it carries little margin for error (Australian Consolidated Press Ltd.)

This is not to be confused with the drop shot, which is far more risky and requires greater control. Instead of being hit deep into the court as stop volleys often are, the drop shot just clears the net to trap your opponent when he is on the base line or behind it. The big risk is that it will not surprise him. If it doesn't you are in trouble, because the drop shot has a high bounce and he has plenty of time to get in to it. One of the smartest times for using the drop shot is immediately after a lob, when your opponent may not have recovered his balance after sprinting back.

A half volley is played immediately after the ball bounces before it rises more than an inch or two. You will have to play it frequently if you are a net-rusher because of the times an opponent will attempt to land the ball at your feet. There is no backswing in the shot—you haven't time for that —and you simply put the string behind the spot where the ball has just bounced. Good timing and footwork is essential, and you shouldn't try it unless you are absolutely compelled to, for the margin of error is high.

The vital factor in smashing the ball that has bounced high on your side of the net is judgment. You have to decide in an instant if it will get up high enough to smash or whether it will be wiser to play a drive as the ball starts to drop. If you try the smash, make sure you bend your knees. Shorten the time it takes to get set for the smash by taking the racket up in front of your body instead of behind it.

Apart from the wonderful opportunity to study these ornaments of the game, I absorbed a tremendous amount of canny tactical dodges on that first overseas tour. Hop taught me particularly that in tennis some points are more important than others. When you are tired, for instance, you have to gather your strength somehow and make a bigger effort on points that will give you a breakthrough or points that will prevent a breakthrough if you win them.

By the time we got to America I was playing far better tennis than I had in Europe, because I was not spoiling my game by trying too hard and because my ground strokes had improved through the enforced rallying for points on European courts. That's why I won the Canadian Junior Singles, and beat Chris Crawford 6–3, 6–3, 6–2 to win the American Junior Championship.

10. That Sunken Chest

It would be ridiculous for a coach to suggest to one of his ordinary pupils who plays the game just for sociability and exercise that he go to the gym to build up his physical equipment. By so doing the coach would almost inevitably ruin the player's interest in the game. This sort of arduous physical preparation is only for the fellow who wants to make tennis his life and to try for the big ones, the fellow who has that restless, nagging desire to be a champion.

There are now, according to some recent figures, more than seven million tennis players in America. I bet not more than a few hundred of them have ever gone into a gym in order to improve their game.

I knew when I was very small that I wanted to be the world's greatest tennis player. As the thrill of rallying on those anthill courts grew, my willingness to work to reach the heights grew too. But I would hate tennis to lose a single player because wearying calisthenics or weight lifting killed his enthusiasm for the sport. This does not mean that even those with limited ambitions in the game will not benefit from simple conditioning exercises.

After the first eye-opening trip overseas in 1956, there was plenty of agitation through the following southern summer for me to be included in the Australian Davis Cup team. Harry Hopman and Queensland officials pressed my claims, but, much to everyone's disappointment at the Shepherds' house in Brisbane, I did not make the team. Instead I got six months' Army training at Wacool camp, quite a bit of it while the best players were off overseas in 1957.

The argument over whether I should be in the Cup team revived again in late 1957. The selectors named five of the six to be included in the team, and I was not among them: Ashley Cooper, Neale Fraser, Bob Mark, Roy Emerson, and Mal Anderson. Everyone in Queensland seemed to think I

had not made it this time because there were two Queens-
landers already in the lineup, Emerson and Anderson.

I appreciated the way my friends and supporters argued
my case, but I knew that even if I got into the team, I would
not play in the Cup matches. I was more concerned with
the chance it would give me to build up my physical resources. In the end the selectors gave me the sixth place
on the team.

This gave me just what I needed to get into peak physical
condition. I had developed a lot since the first day Harry
Hopman saw me slouched against the wire fence at Milton,
but I still had to get power into my chest and shoulders and
improve my breathing. I had worked out at Snowy Hill's
gymnasium at Brisbane. Now I got the chance in the Cup
squad to follow a conditioning course mapped out by Hop
and Stan Nicholes, head masseur at the Melbourne gym that
Frank Sedgman later bought.

When I started, my routine included work with the heavy
weights, dumbbells, trunk bending over the incline-board,
bike pedaling, wrist curls, jackknives, and pull-ups in which
I pulled my chin above the level of a bar I could reach only
by jumping. Later I forgot about the heavy weights, concentrating instead on improving my agility, loosening my
muscles, and speeding up my reflexes. But the exercises I
had to concentrate on were specially worked out to build
up my chest development.

Nicholes studies each player, and works out a schedule
that will help his personal physical deficiencies. Hoad, when
he first went to Nicholes, was already built like a longshore-
man, so he was given exercises to make him whippy and
increase his speed. Sedgman had speed and those wonderful
reflexes, but he needed building up in the chest to increase
his stamina. Among younger players Margaret Smith has
improved her all-round game by going regularly to Nicholes's gym when she is at home.

When you are away from the courts, training at a gym-

Laver and his 1961 Davis Cup squad mates (left to right: Neale Fraser, Rod Laver, Ken Fletcher, Harry Hopman, Bob Hewitt, Fred Stolle, and Roy Emerson). Note how strong each one of these players is in the legs

nasium or running round the local football oval is usually
your own responsibility. Start by taking a hard look at yourself in the mirror. If you are too bulky, then you will need
weight-reducing work. If you legs are frail, you can build
them up by pedaling and plenty of running. You will soon
discover where your body needs development, but always
remember that in tennis you do not require powerful muscles. Tennis players seldom run further to get the ball than
ten yards. They need fast reflexes, trim bodies without any
excess weight, coordination, chests that permit free breathing for prolonged periods, and wiry, streamlined legs.
Weight lifting without expert supervision can be very
harmful.

If you aim to be a champion, buy yourself a track suit
and get out two or three times a week and try simple conditioning exercises. Alternate the routine if you begin to lose
interest. Make sure that the exercises you do include plenty
of stretching, such as toe-touching and side-bending. Soon
you will feel a lot better physically, and you will not lose
your wind at the vital stage of a match.

In the Davis Cup workouts I found Ashley Cooper one of
the hardest workers. "Coop" confessed he had been a fat
boy as a child, and he knew that his heavy legs needed lots
of running if he was to compete on equal terms with the
American team in the Challenge Round. He ran round and
round an oval in a heavy track suit, suddenly sprinting for
ten to fifteen yards, pulling up, and then jogging again
until the next sudden sprint. At the start of the season he
went out on the road for runs of up to ten miles.

For two or three weeks before the Challenge Round, Hop
had us out every day for a run and some exercises. There was
always plenty of ginger in what we did. We would run
through a park, then stop to do some double knee jumps,
press-ups or star jumps, but never attempting the exercises
until we were properly warmed up. The double knee jump
has become a trademark of Australian Cup teams. It is

An Australian Davis Cup squad goes through its paces at training. It is often said that under Coach Hopman the Australian teams are peppier, sounder in wind and limb than at any time in their careers. Often the same players decline when left to train themselves (*Herald-Sun Photograph, Melbourne*)

simple to do: you leap into the air from a standing position, and at the highest point of the jump you bend both knees and tug them in to your chest. Immediately you land you repeat it and you go on doing it until you have to quit. Don Candy holds the Cup team record of ninety-three double knee jumps. Most of the boys get to seventy before they have to stop. The star jump is merely a jump in which you throw out your arms and legs to form the four points of a star when you are at your peak height.

I had already discovered that Hop believed in exercises to strengthen the stomach muscles, reasoning that if you were well tuned up around the midriff you would breathe better and never become exhausted on the court.

Every member of the team went through these condition-

ing exercises, and those who knew they would not play in the Cup worked just as hard to get those who would into the best shape possible. It is valuable for all—not only No. 1 and No. 2 players—to be able to place a ball wherever Hop asks, when practicing for the Cup. One year Bob Mark served literally hundreds of balls to Neale Fraser's backhand because Hop wanted to give Fraser a return of serve that would not break down. Fraser enormously improved his return of service, and Mark got so expert he could serve to a left-hander's backhand in his sleep.

Through all of these Davis Cup campaigns Hop kept pushing home to us the necessity for good healthy food and lots of rest. The team always showed up at social engagements splendidly fitted out, but never stayed very late. We had no set diet, but we ate lots of fruit and stayed away from starchy foods and any kind of alcohol.

Women tennis players have to accept the fact that they cannot run as well as the men. Their lack of speed in covering the court is the main reason why women's tennis is an altogether different game from the one men play. Very few women have the mobility to play the net game favored by most of the world's leading men players. When a girl can run well enough to get to the net often—as Margaret Smith can—then she is in a good position to create havoc among her opponents.

I have sometimes been asked to take a look at a promising girl player and suggest ways of improving her game. Usually I find that the girl has well-produced strokes but that she is so big in the hips that she cannot get to the ball to play it. The only answer is a program of exercises that will cut ten

This shot of Ken Rosewall reaching for a volley clearly demonstrates the value of a powerful forearm (United Press Photos)

pounds or more from her weight. However, not many girls are prepared to stick to these exercises.

You hear plenty of talk around the tournaments about relaxation. Very few players below the top rank understand what this means. Tennis is one of the few games in which you have to concentrate intently and relax at the same time. Nobody can possibly hope to concentrate at a high pitch for the three hours some matches take. The answer is to concentrate when you are playing the points but to relax between games, while the ballboys are collecting the balls.

The 1958 Challenge Round—the first ever played in my adopted home city of Brisbane—was spectacular and dramatic from the first serve until the last point, when America took the Cup from us by winning the first singles played on the final day. We had a strong, fit team, but it performed far below its capabilities, and this enabled Peruvian-born Alex Olmedo to dominate the match.

Mal Anderson lost the opening singles to Olmedo, then Ashley Cooper tied it up for Australia by beating Barry MacKay. Next day America recovered from a two-sets-to-love deficit to win a really great doubles that Australia narrowly missed taking in straight sets.

One of the strangest sights on any tennis court that day was the behavior of the American team. The match lasted for four hours and four minutes of play, and went through eighty-two games. It was, of course, a harrowing match for captain Perry Jones. None of the players could have lasted in that tropical heat if they had not been superbly fit. Before Olmedo and Ham Richardson defeated Anderson and Fraser 10–12, 3–6, 16–14, 6–3, 7–5, Jones had exhausted himself, dancing on the courtside, applauding American winners until his hands were sore, imitating linesmen's signals, and shouting advice to his players everyone in the capacity crowd could hear. At the end of the match the marks in the turf around Jones's chair were as bumpy as any out on the court where all four players wore spikes.

With America leading two matches to one, Cooper went out to play Olmedo on the final day in an incredibly tense atmosphere. The crowd was so excited it could not control its reactions, and the referee, Cliff Sproule, repeatedly had to go to the microphone and ask for silence during the rallies. Sproule's hands shook, and his voice croaked from strain as he did it.

Cooper, due to be married two days later, was so nervous that the tennis balls stuck in his hand as he tried to toss them up to serve. Olmedo's weakness was supposed to be his backhand, but when Cooper served to it Olmedo kept running round it and taking the ball off his forehand. This tactic completely upset Cooper's serving rhythm, and Olmedo won 6–3, 4–6, 6–4, 8–6.

As I watched Olmedo win the Cup for his team I realized that the next year he would be the man to beat in all the big events. He was remarkably fit, with a tremendous pair of legs that had stood up to nine muscle-tearing hours on spikes—which he had never worn before. I ached for the chance to be part of Australia's bid to get the Cup back. The best way to make sure I was in the team that would follow the Cup to America next year was to work even harder and to make certain I was in the best shape of my life.

11. To the Net with the Right Man

If you want to play winning tennis, you must get it into your head at the very beginning that to play good doubles requires an entirely different tactical approach from singles. Teamwork is the open secret of success in doubles, and it can only come from regular play with your partner and an appreciation of the need to work in a pattern. If your partner drops back, go back with him. If you go to the net, go in together. One up and one back in a rally creates a gap that enables your opposition to win a point without even trying.

When I lived in Brisbane I always liked to play doubles with Frank Gorman. Poor Frank had worrying family troubles, but he seldom showed it on the court. Nevertheless, although we won the Australian Junior Doubles one year, for one reason or another his tennis did not improve as fast as mine did. He did not get away on an overseas trip until 1958 when a group of friends raised a fund to which Queensland tennis fans subscribed. Halfway through the trip, he got so homesick he went home to Queensland.

On my own first overseas trip I played doubles with Bob Mark, but we did not make a good combination. Mark liked the second court, where I always played because I was left-handed, and he never really settled down on the first court. He was rated a good doubles player because he had such a great return of service, but in the highest class of doubles he hit the ball too hard to win. In doubles, you must slow your game down a fraction to increase your

Modern doubles is a game of fast volleys at the net, well-angled and powerfully hit smashes. Reflexes play a crucial part as matches usually are won by the team which shows the most aggression (left, Laver; right, Mark) (United Press Photos)

accuracy, and keep the ball low. Hitting it as powerfully as you do in singles pushes up your quota of errors and lifts the ball higher over the net so that your opponents can get a crack at volleying it away.

Doubles has a fascination missing from singles provided you have the right partner with you to enjoy it and, I may add, to win. You get a kick out of coordinating your shots with a good partner. Great Australian pairs like Adrian Quist and John Bromwich or Frank Sedgman and Ken Mc-Gregor are classic examples of this vital team effort. Bromwich made the openings for Quist to volley and smash away winners. McGregor was a perfect foil for Sedgman.

Towards the end of my amateur career I was lucky to partner Roy Emerson. He was ideal for me. He was a splendid first court player, and he had the essential knack of keeping the ball low and slowing his shots down slightly. He always hit his volleys away from the man at the net.

Whoever you pick for your doubles partner should complement you, mentally as well as in stroke play. There have been one or two doubles pairs who continually quarreled, but they were very rare or very gifted. You should get on well with your partner to have any hope of winning.

The trick of winning in modern doubles is to dominate the net. It demands crisp volleying without any chop in order to keep the ball low over the net, fast reflexes, and an ability to smash and lob with judgment.

If you can get to the net before your opponents, you must eventually triumph. For this reason it is important to use the full advantage of serving by getting your first service into play. Slow your service down a little and make sure you hit it deep. This will enable you to follow the ball to the net. If you miss your first service, the receiver is likely to step in closer and attack your second service, following it to the net first. Try to get ninety per cent of your first serves into play. In doubles, double faults are an absolute crime.

In serving, you can move nearer the side lines than in

singles, where you take up a position near the center line.
I generally serve in doubles from a spot close to the inter-
section of the singles-court side line and the base line. This
wider position gives me more angle on my service, and
means I can hit the ball harder because I will have a bigger
distance to the receiver's court than if I stand near the
center line.

They say that Bromwich could go through a whole doubles match without missing a single return of service. I have
seen Mal Anderson with his wonderful return of service
come pretty close to doing this, but I do not think I have
ever seen anyone with Bromwich's ability to drop his returns right at the toes of the server as he tried to move into
the net. Control your return of service so that you hit it
cross-court and low without setting up an easy volley for
the man at the net or the server. Keep the ball low and, by
punching the volley, make it difficult for the server to get
to the net. Don't try for returns of service down the side
line unless you think the net man is moving too far into the
server's court, trying to poach your return.

The essential point to remember when you rush the net
with your partner is that a lob over your head will seldom
produce an outright winner. You can usually get back to a
lob and return it. The other factor working for you when
you move to the net is that it is always difficult to smash
through two players.

Before you start your first match together have a few
words with your doubles partner about basic tactics. In par-
ticular, discuss where you will both stand, on service and
receiving service. Most Australian doubles teams play with
one man at the net and the other covering the base-line
formation. American pairs frequently play with both players
in the rear of the court. This is a purely defensive formation
with which to begin a point. You will not get as much pleasure out of a doubles match standing back swapping ground
drives as you will by moving to the net. Standing back, you

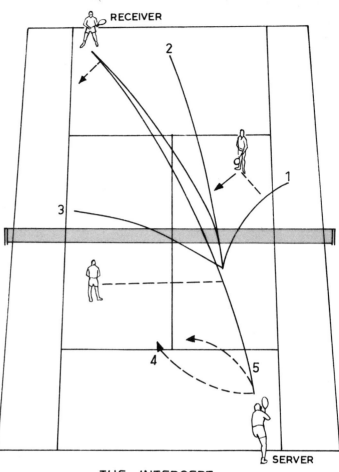

RECEIVER

SERVER

THE INTERCEPT

have to win on ground-stroke errors. Up front, you can volley away your opponents' returns and enjoy a little intercepting and poaching.

Here are the telltale differences between an outstanding doubles pair and a moderate combination:

The good pair always chips to the feet of the server away from the net man, and follows the chip to the net.

Facing a good pair, the net man seldom gets into the game. They will have the knack of keeping the ball away from him.

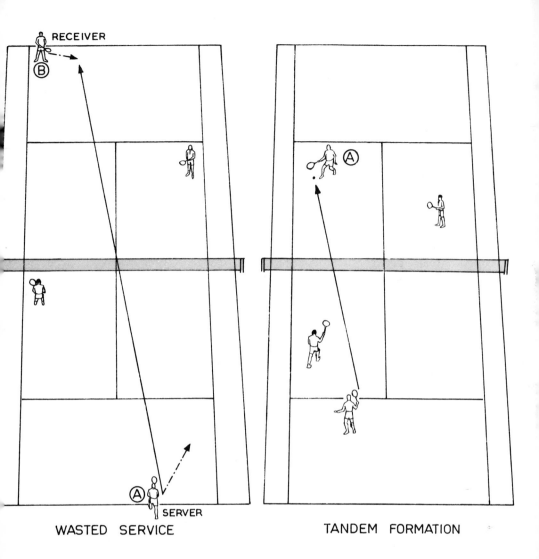

RECEIVER

B

A

SERVER

WASTED SERVICE

TANDEM FORMATION

(Opposite) *The intercept most commonly used in doubles is made by the man at the net when a strong service from his partner draws a weak return. The server moves to the net along path 4 on a signaled poach and up path 5 on an unsignaled poach. Positions 1, 2, and 3 show possible placements of the interceptor's volley*

(Above, left) *The server has wasted a strong first service by failing to follow it to the net. This sketch shows how much more court the receiver (B) now has to aim at with the server (A) hanging on the base line*

(Above, right) *The tandem formation requires both players in a team to stand on the same side of the court. This prevents an opponent using a powerful shot. Player A has to forgo his favorite backhand and try to return the ball into the empty spaces with his suspect forehand*

When they cannot spot an empty space into which to put the ball, the good pair volleys straight at an opponent at the net.

The good pair never serves double faults, and almost always gets their first serve in.

The good pair never tries to be too smart for their own good or keeps trying for freakish angles. They prefer to put their first volley down the center and create an opening for their second volleys.

The bad pair does not understand that in doubles the lob can be an offensive shot, especially if it is well concealed.

The bad pair is wide open to an occasional shot down the side line because the net man edges towards the center chasing intercepts, and leaves his side of the court unguarded.

The bad team always seems to be bustled out of their normal shotmaking rhythm by the crowding tactics of a good pair, who nevertheless continue to play at a fraction below their singles speed.

Australia has lost the Davis Cup three times since 1950, and on each occasion the loss of the Doubles proved the decisive factor. That is why we place such importance on the Doubles in Australia. Our players have won ten out of the first sixteen Wimbledon's Men's Doubles titles since 1946. At Adelaide in 1963, Australia's lack of a first-rate doubles pair for the first time in a decade meant she couldn't get the doubles point she needed to go with Roy Emerson's two singles points. America won 3–2.

The doubles match at Brisbane in 1958 about which I have written in the last chapter swung on the Americans' clever use of the tandem formation. Serving to Neale Fraser, both Olmedo and Richardson stood on the same side of the court, inviting Fraser to return the ball down the side line, a shot with which he had far more trouble than on his cross-court return. The Americans did not adopt this tandem formation on every serve, only on every two or three points, and this uncertainty about when it would be used helped to upset Fraser's splendid touch. This was perfect use of the tandem, designed to prevent an opponent using a dangerous shot. Fraser had worried Olmedo and Richardson with a chipped cross-court return throughout the first two sets.

At Sydney in 1954, Seixas and Trabert defeated Hoad and Rosewall in four sets by using a signaling technique that broke up the Australians' concentration. As the Americans were about to serve, the man at the net would turn, and, by the way he placed his fingers on the racket or some other signal, indicate the tactics for the next rally. Their main signal set up the use of the scissors, by which the net man moved to cover the cross-court return while the server moved quickly to cover the down–the–line return instead of going to the net. The scissors calls for split-second timing, but Seixas and Trabert managed to bring it off frequently— probably because they had rehearsed it in training.

Tennis buffs all over the world often ask me if I approve of these signaling systems in doubles, and my answer is always the same—I do not think they are necessary if you are a good pair. Whether the signaling is sportsmanlike depends on how it is used. If it holds up play and is meant to upset the concentration of a rival pair when stroke play cannot do it, then it is distinctly unfair. But in a game in which it is possible to exchange words with your partner that linesmen cannot hear, it makes no sense to make up codes or to signal behind your back or by your grip on the racket what the next stratagem should be.

There is no doubt that the sight of Seixas or Trabert at the

(p. 116-117) *An aerial view of the doubles between Alex Olmedo– Ham Richardson, of the United States, and Mal Anderson–Neale Fraser, of Australia, which decided the 1958 Davis Cup Challenge Round in favor of the United States. The Americans' clever use of the tandem formation when serving to Fraser's backhand was the factor which helped them win* (Australian News and Information Bureau)

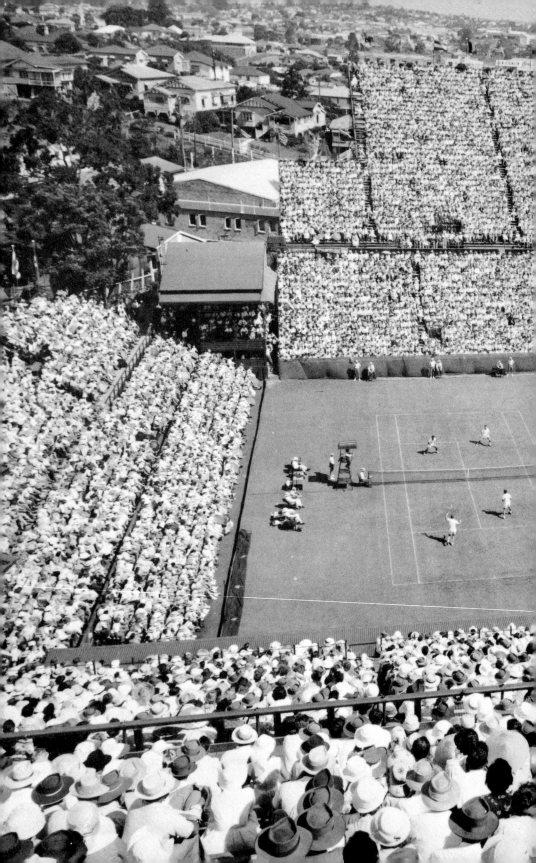

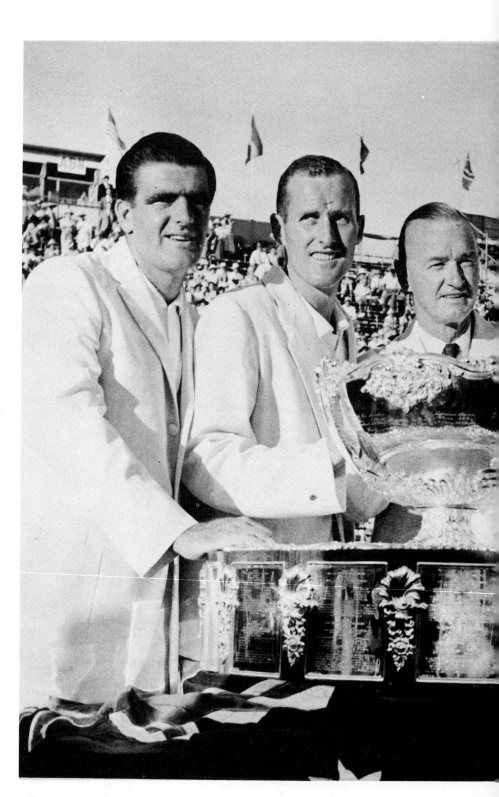

The winning Australian Davis Cup team poses before the Cup in 1961 (left to right: Bob Mark, Neale Fraser, Harry Hopman, Rod Laver, and Roy Emerson)

net signaling to his partner as he was about to serve upset Hoad and Rosewall. But it did not cause the Australians' defeat as much as their shotmaking weaknesses and their refusal to take chances.

When we left Australia in the 1959 official Australian team to try and bring the Davis Cup back, we knew we had two experienced doubles teams to rely on for the Challenge Round, provided we got that far. With Anderson and Cooper turned professional, our top pair were Roy Emerson and Neale Fraser, and for the second pair, myself and Bob Mark.

Davis Cup doubles, with a full day devoted to the match, is one thing. Tournament doubles, in which you may draw two or three matches on the same day if you play in both mixed and men's, is altogether different. When I got to the Wimbledon final in 1959 to play Alex Olmedo I had played almost eight hundred games in five days because of my doubles commitments, a total so high that it worried the soul out of Charlie Hollis listening to the match on the radio back home.

12. "One Darn Winner After Another!"

At Wimbledon that year Alex Olmedo was a fast mover with a fine, easy service swing and well-controlled volleys. He and I met in the finals. He based his game on commanding the net. His ground strokes were not exceptional, but they were sound enough to serve him on the few occasions when he was not at the net. To beat him I had to get to the net first and pressure his backhand, which was the weakest shot in his game.

I had to keep him stretching and keep the ball at his feet as he came in to volley so that he would have to keep hitting half volleys. I also had to keep angling the ball across him so that I had a good chance of passing him as often as he put away a winning volley. Most of all, I had to serve at least as well as he did.

On the crucial day I failed to do most of these things; I was very nervous, although I may not have shown it. This, coupled with all the tennis I had played in the ten days before we met, took the edge from my game, and I was tired. This takes nothing away from Alex, who won the final 6–4, 6–3, 6–4 in seventy-one minutes. I do not say I would have won had I been fresher, but I know I would have given him a tougher match if I had not played so many long matches in the days before.

Gardnar Mulloy, one of the most experienced players in the game, told the English newspapers, "Olmedo had it easy because MacKay softened Rod up. That was what really killed Rod." Barry MacKay and I had played for more than three hours in the semifinals two days earlier before I scraped home 11–13, 11–9, 10–8, 7–9, 6–3. We started in midafternoon, and had a tremendous struggle until nearly dark. In the fifth set MacKay led 3–1, and my chances of getting to the final seemed hopeless. I told myself not to panic, to keep trying, and not to play safe. Suddenly, all my shots started to go in, and I reeled off five games in a row to get through to the Olmedo match.

"The match was mine. I had it won, and he stole it from me. How? He just hit one darn winner after another. There was nothing I could do about them." This was how MacKay described my match against him. My instinctive approach that I must always go for my shots paid off. If I could have played as well in the finals, I might have won.

Olmedo had had a fantastic seven months of tennis climaxed by his win at Wimbledon. Just before the Challenge Round at the end of December in Australia he had been just another good amateur. There was even a lot of criticism of his selection on the United States team: many Americans considered him ineligible because of his Peruvian birth. Most of the writers said Ham Richardson should not have lost his singles berth to Olmedo. Whatever the merits of the question, Olmedo grabbed his chance. He was the hero of the Davis Cup victory for America, and only seven months later he had beaten me to capture Wimbledon. Even playing at your very best it is difficult to break down the game of a player enjoying such a great run of success. I had had stretches of tennis myself when every shot I hit was a world-beater, when everything I tried came off, and even the shots I hit off the wood were winners.

Olmedo gave a perfect display of the net-rushing game. His booming service was very hard to get back, let alone keep low at his feet. This allowed him to dictate the match from the net and keep me running. I was repeatedly out of court as he knocked off a winner at the net. His pressure forced me to make my shots hurriedly, and increased my errors.

Laver has played a passing shot as opponent Neale Fraser crowds the net and both now watch the outcome of the stroke. Note the space that was open to Laver in aiming this shot

I got to all three finals that year at Wimbledon, but won only one of them, the Mixed Doubles with Darlene Hard. Bob Mark and I lost the Doubles to Emerson and Fraser in four sets. In the twelve days I played 628 games, and Wimbledon officials said they thought this was a record for one player in the tournament. Charles Hollis and some of my admirers back home said I was crazy to play in all three events and felt that I should have concentrated on the Singles. But I loved to play so much that I was willing to accept even these exhausting doubles matches just before the Singles final.

I soaked up a tremendous amount of experience that year. After Wimbledon we went down to Mexico for the Davis Cup matches. I played singles for Australia with Neale Fraser. In my first match I just could not handle the conditions at that altitude, and Mario Llamas beat me in three sets. Fraser made it 1–all, and then won the doubles with Emerson to give us a 2–1 lead. Before we started the final day, Fraser had an attack of appendicitis, so it was vital that I clinch the tie by beating Tony Palafox and prevent Fraser having to play the fifth and deciding match in such a weakened condition. At one stage, when I was down two sets to one, even my teammates gave up hope. Fraser and Emerson went out to get Neale warmed up on an outside court. But I recovered to win in five sets. It was closer than the scores showed, as Neale had taken five sets to win his opening singles and might have been in real trouble had he got into a long match to decide the tie.

Hopman kept me in the team as a singles player against Cuba, India, and Italy—where I beat Nicola Pietrangeli— and against the United States in the Challenge Round. Few people realize the extra strain involved in Davis Cup matches. You feel your responsibility the moment the umpire calls "Australia" instead of calling out your name, as he would in an ordinary tournament. In a tournament you are playing only for yourself, but in the Davis Cup you play for your country, and trying not to fail in this trust really builds up the tension. That is why it is always handy to have Harry Hopman around to encourage you. He did not say much, just enough to keep you on the job, "Aim for the lines more," or "Hit your serve—don't pat it."

It had become a habit for me to start my singles matches so casually that I seemed to lose my first service automatically. In fact, I was such a bad starter that in our seven-week struggle to get the Davis Cup back, Hoppy and I seriously discussed giving up the right to serve first when I won the toss, an important advantage to most top amateurs. Hoppy kept saying that there was no "killer" in me, and I guess I proved he was right by the way I kept losing my service immediately after managing to get a service break. The answer was to think more about my game, and to me this came slowly, very slowly.

Luckily for Australia, Fraser was not as casual as I was, and in the Challenge Round he got the Cup back for Australia by winning both his singles and taking the Doubles with Emerson. I lost both my singles, but in the second match did a lot better against Olmedo than at Wimbledon. Alex won this time 9–7, 4–6, 10–8, 12–10, and it took him three hours and twenty minutes to do it. My lack of experience in knowing what to do on the big points spoiled my chances. You can play brilliant shots with the score 15–all, but it is at 40–30, or deuce and your advantage, when brilliance counts.

Tennis players fall neatly into certain categories, depending on how they approach a singles match. I knew by this time what I had to do against any given type of opposition, and Hoppy said I had the strokes to do it, but I had to cut down on my errors and get that casual streak out of my system.

On paper, here are the basic rules for winning singles:

1. Hit the ball away from your opponent, into the gaps and not to him unless you mean it as a surprise. You achieve this largely by hitting for the lines. Learn to put the ball where you aim it.

2. Remember that the net is an even bigger obstacle than your opponent. Most of your errors will end up in the net.

3. Don't change your game because you get into trouble with an opponent who hits a few winners. Play your natural style, whether you rely on volleying at the net, use an all-court game, or like to rally from the base line.

4. Practice the trick of setting up points with your service. You do not need a big service to do this, provided you can control it and keep it deep. Serves which draw your rival out of court will do the job just as effectively as cannonball serves.

5. However hopeless your position, keep trying.

6. Make sure your physical fitness matches the demands of the class of tennis you play. Mastery of all the shots is useless if you cannot get into position to make them. Good physical condition is the best way of all of beating the tension which reduces many good players to shambling wrecks.

7. Concentrate hard on the big points to give yourself every chance of making a great shot. The ability to hit great shots in a crisis has made national champions out of many players with quite ordinary strokes.

8. Think about your game. Don't become an automaton with good strokes. You can start by taking a look at your opponent's game before you meet him, and then sit down to work out ways of beating him.

I constantly relearned all these points as I toured with the 1959 Australia cup-winning team. We would sit down with pencil and paper working out how to angle shots away from players we were about to meet. Tactics were our standard

After the shot let him down in one of his early professional matches, Laver examines each part of his forehand, trying to work out what is causing the trouble. The first thing is to get that front foot across the body

conversation, whether we were in cabs, aeroplanes, buses, or playing a game of checkers in a hotel room. It is the only way to learn the know-how that makes a champion, but to acquire it you have to go over the fundamental tactics of the game again and again and again.

Adrian Quist, the famous Australian Davis Cup player who has become one of the most thoughtful critics of the game, always says that the ultimate in tennis is to develop the all-court game. I agree with him. The net-rushing game and the base-line game can be effective, but, as Adrian says, the big achievement is to be able to play at the top of your game from anywhere on the court.

NET-RUSHING: the percentages favor this approach in singles because so few players develop the control required to play consistently good lobs and passing shots.

Go to the net in threatening fashion. Try to hurry your opponent into mistakes. Put the pressure on him to make a great shot—but don't get in too close. Go in on a flat shot that is deep to your opponent's base line. This will keep the ball lower than a top-spin shot and let you get in closer. A flat shot also will keep lower and force your opponent to bend lower and hit it upwards. Keep your top spin for passing shots or base-line exchanges. To counter a net-rusher, keep the ball at his feet, and try to angle the ball across his body.

BASE-LINE STRATEGY: if your game depends on good ground strokes, you must also depend on achieving good length with your drives. Learn to conceal the direction of your shots so as to keep a net-rusher guessing. Don't get discouraged if he puts away some of your lobs; your lobs may be taking the sting from his stroking and wearing him down.

Counter a base-liner by mixing up the pace of your shots. Give him top spin and, occasionally, sliced as well as flat drives. This will break up his rhythm and spoil his timing. If he has not got a big serve, attack it, following your return

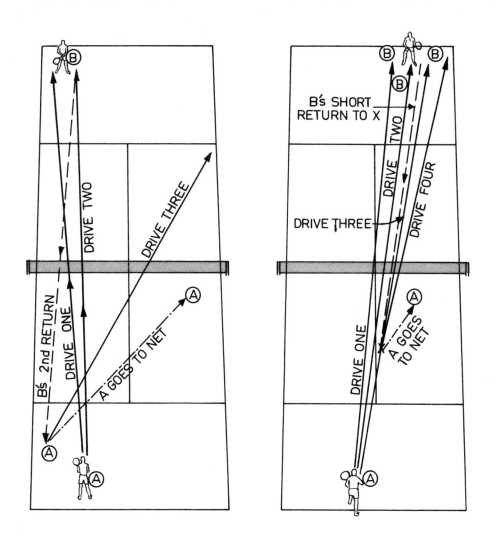

(Left) *Player A sustains his attack with two drives deep to B's forehand. The return from the second drive is weak, so A hammers it sharply across court and moves to the net. This means B has to hit a perfect passing shot on the run or lob over A or lose the point as A volleys away his return*

(Right) *This time A attacks B's backhand, striking three heavy drives deep to the base line. This compels B to return weakly to the point marked X. Sustaining the pressure, A puts this back deep into the backhand corner, advancing to the net to put away the return*

to the net. If he has a heavy serve, wait for the short one and then go to the net behind a good deep shot. Don't sacrifice length for speed.

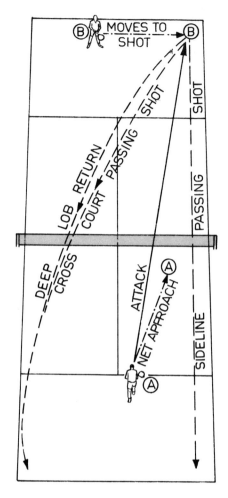

(Left to right) *BACKHAND ATTACK:* From midcourt, player A has driven deep into B's backhand corner and has followed to the net. This leaves B with the alternatives of playing a high lob over A's head, a cross-court passing shot, or a down-the-line passing shot

FOREHAND ATTACK: This time A has attacked the forehand, driving deep to the base line and following to the net. Again B has to decide among a deep lob, a cross-court passing shot, or a side-line passing shot

Many accomplished volleyers play down the middle of their opponent's court, thus reducing the angle their rival can get onto his next shot. Drives to the backhand have been labeled A and B, and those to the forehand, C and D. The shot down the center is labeled E. Constant pressure is the secret

The finest tennis players of all are those who can combine the net-rushing and the base-line game, players who can go to the net to win a point with a volley or smash or stay back to win it with a lob or a passing shot. There are very few players in the world today who can do this. All of them are in professional tennis. In amateur tennis, the players who keep going to the net generally win, except on very slow services in Europe where you have to rally from the base line because you cannot put the ball away as easily as on grass, boards, or concrete.

We were a very happy group when we reached Los Angeles on our way back home to Australia in 1959. We had

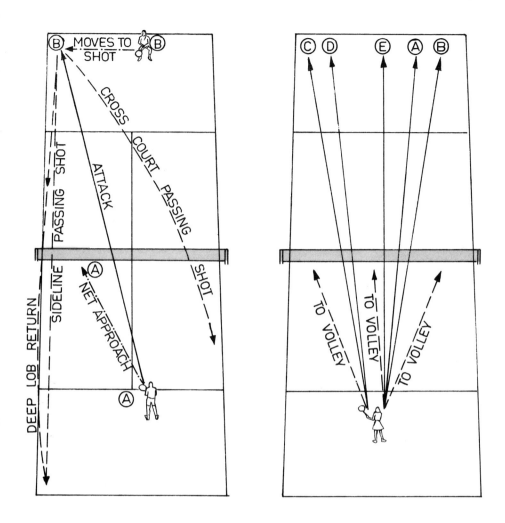

won back the Davis Cup, and Neale Fraser had followed his
Cup success by winning the United States Singles. We had
done it by sticking to the sound tactical principles which I
have outlined in this chapter.

13. When Nothing Works

The net seems yards higher, the court smaller, the ball won't land where you aim it. It happens to even the greatest players; they cannot seem to get their game going. When this has happened to me I try to get back to Rockhampton to see Charlie Hollis or to Brisbane to Ian Ayre to have my tennis overhauled.

I had been in Australia's Davis Cup team for two years, and there were still faults in my stroke production. When I lost five finals in a row, I went back to Rockhampton for a cure. I got up at five that first morning just as I had in the old days, and Charlie Hollis took me out on to the crushed anthill court. After we had hit a few, he said: "Where's the spin I taught you? Whatever happened to all that top spin everybody was talking about?"

I was trying for so much extra power that I had fallen into the habit of hitting every ball flat. This had taken the spin from my game and cut down my ability to put the ball where I wanted it. Moreover, it meant I had given up the game I had learned to be able to offset the big men's power. Charlie put my game together again by slowing down my strokes. Next day I went out and played Frank Gorman in the Central Queensland Singles final, and beat him 6–0, 6–1 in about a quarter of an hour. "What did you do to him, Charlie—hit him with a needle?" asked Frank.

Charlie was still annoyed with me because I had let myself in for those long doubles matches at Wimbledon. "Don't play mixed doubles again," he said. "Be smart like the top guys and concentrate on winning the Singles. Nobody cares if you win all the mixed doubles ever played. Win the Wimbledon Singles, and the whole world knows your name. I will say you look fit. That wrist really has developed well."

"I ought to look fit—Hoppy runs the guts out of us."

Largely because of Hopman and the joshing from Charlie Hollis I was beginning to think more about what I was doing on a tennis court. This meant that when my strokes were wildly sprayed, I was trying to find a solution. When I got in with a fellow whose game worried me, I was more likely to work out a counter.

The first thing to do when all your efforts towards mastering the game and its tactics collapse is to go off by yourself and quietly analyze possible reasons. Are you taking your eye off the ball? Are you getting that opposite-side foot across so that you hit the ball when you're side-on to the net? Are you trying to hit it harder than you should with your build? Is your backswing wrong? Most of all, though, take a hard look at your grips.

When you think you have the answer to your troubles, coax another player to go out and hit a few balls with you so that you can work out your errors. The greatest players in the world are never afraid of drilling the mistakes from their game on the practice court.

You can go mentally stale if you have played too much tennis. If it is impossible to rest from tournament play, change your habits. Try to find some fresh off-the-court interests. On their first overseas trips a lot of young players get very homesick. I know that I suffered from it. It is a strange disease, and it usually affected me when I was losing matches I thought I should have won. A few good wins soon convinced me that the traveling around was worthwhile after all.

One year Queensland fans of Frank Gorman got up a fund to send him overseas for a few months with Bob Hewitt, who was subsidized by a similar fund in New South Wales. Frank had only been away a short time, and had hardly given himself a chance to settle down when he got a case of homesickness. In a twinkling he decided to fly home from Europe to Brisbane amid some very angry but justified

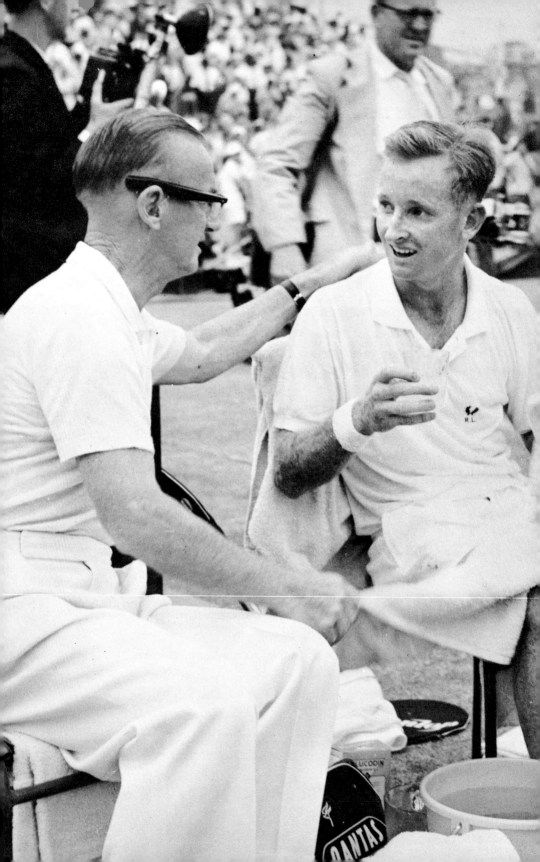

blasts from his supporters. It was typical of Gorman's act-first, think-later temperament, but for all that you could not help but sympathize with him.

The amateur circuit today presents just about every known problem for an ambitious young player. Until he gains the proper experience he can watch his game go to pieces, with a thirty-mile-an-hour wind blowing down the court as it does at Barranquilla, or against an opponent who in all fairness does not have a shot to his name but keeps getting the ball back. There are dozens of such players in every continental tournament.

Lack of concentration is a frequent cause of a good stroke makeup going wrong. As an amateur I always found my concentration was better at the end of a really grueling five-setter than in the first few games. I liked to begin slowly and get all my shots working. Then I could go faster later on. If I began with a rush, my game never coordinated, and I was terrible. Sometimes I got so far behind I did not dare to look at the scoreboard. If I had, I would have seen how near I was to losing, and this would have taken my mind off the business of good, strong shotmaking, which in the end is what makes a champion.

In 1960 I had a fantastic match with Fraser to win my first major title, the Australian Singles, held that year in Brisbane. I fought off match point in the fourth set, and in the last game of the fifth set Fraser saved six match points and twice had a point to break my serve. When you lead 7–6 and 40–love on your own serve after three hours in the heat, and the other fellow gets up to deuce and then has advan-

Coach Harry Hopman congratulates Laver after a Davis Cup Challenge Round win. In Davis Cup, coaches can advise players at each change of ends; at Wimbledon and in the other major tournaments, they are on their own

tage point, it is really exciting. The crowd was nearly hysterical through that last game, but I scraped home 5–7, 3–6, 6–3, 8–6, 8–6. I knew then that I was on my way to the big time. I had broken through at last.

Worrying about your nearness to defeat or your opponent's big strokes can completely upset your rhythm. Perhaps that is why I had trouble gauging Fraser's different services in the 1960 Wimbledon final. It was my second successive final, and I should have been confident after my Australian win, but I could not spot his kicker from his flat serve often enough to win. I knew the watch was going to be tough, and fretting about it did not help. This time Fraser won, and he did it again in the United States final that year at Forest Hills.

For me, the tactical challenge in playing Fraser hung entirely on whether I could break his service. He hardly had a ground shot to call his own. I had to be able to stand in and attack his serve to get the break that would win a set, and at the same time I had to serve well enough to hold my own delivery. He got such fantastic spin on the ball by arching his back that this may have aggravated his troubles with his legs.

When I was not playing in the big tournaments I still lived in Brisbane, working at the Dunlop office and living at my second home, the Shepherds' house in Koala Road, Moorooka. For practice and improvement, I tried to get away for two or three lunch hours each week to work with Ian Ayre on the shots that were not getting results. Usually Frank Gorman and I went together. Ian charged us a purely nominal amount for the practice and coaching, and he did this only because he felt that by doing so we would try a little harder. These sessions were immensely helpful in improving my tactical equipment. Frank and I would play a set or two. Both of us really wanted to win. Every few games Ian would stop us, and explain why we should have played certain points differently.

I was now getting a little more from Dunlop than my original salary, but I was in no sense rolling in money. A lot of nonsense has been written about my salary from Dunlop; I have seen it quoted at £A2,000 ($4,480) a year. I certainly did not get that much. The association with a firm like Dunlop pays off best in trips to tournaments without loss of pay. Most firms give a bonus of £A100 ($224) if you win a national title like the Australian or United States Singles, £A200 ($448) for winning Wimbledon, but you get so busy playing tennis you seldom stop to think about whether it is worth more pay. Tennis was such an important part of my life I would have played for nothing if I had to.

It is true that good amateurs, if they are lucky, can make £A100 ($224) or more a tournament, plus expenses, on the South American and European circuits. But it is not because he has anything to spare out of this that a player stays on the circuit. Part of it is the pleasant life, but mainly he is in it because he is a competitor working on his game trying to get that backhand or forehand right or learning how to beat the other fellow to the net. I never did feel any moral obligations in being an amateur, and I am sure none of the leading players is concerned at all by the stories about "hypocrisy." The players did not create the system; they simply go along with it.

On the 1960 world tour I was lucky to have Adrian Quist as team manager. Adrian was in the Australian team that won the 1939 Davis Cup from the United States after losing the first two matches. He and John Bromwich won at Wimbledon in 1950 when they were thought to be long past their best. So I had someone to whom I could talk every night after the matches, someone who knew from thirty years' experience how titles are won. The important point, I think, is that all the men who had some part in building up my game—Charlie Hollis, Ian Ayre, Harry Hopman, Adrian Quist—were men who could go out and hit the ball with me, men who knew from close up what I was doing wrong.

This is where other countries make a mistake in challenging Australia's supremacy: they send as team managers, non-players who can never really get close to their team, however hard they try.

Sometimes on tour Adrian would roast me for trying to hit winners off every ball that came to me or for failing to concentrate or for always trying for a brilliant shot when an easier one would have won the point. Sometimes I would get really hot for six or eight games, but I could not sustain it for three sets or more. Yet I kept trying, always attempting to belt the ball with a good, fluent stroke and never playing safe.

I always took my track suit along wherever I went, and when I felt sour on the world or my game was not working, I would slip into my suit and go for a run. The sweat would roll off me and so would my bad temper.

In 1961, I began the year thinking I might have a chance of a Grand Slam. Fraser was fading because of his bad knee, and I was maturing all the time, mentally and in my stroke production. I came undone, however, in the very first tournament in the Slam when I hurt my wrist. I was lucky to get through to the final against Emerson, and I had to play it with two matchboxes bound round my wrist, held in place by adhesive tape. I had to hit every ball flat. My wrist was too painful for me to play my normal game, and finally I could not use my wrist at all. Emerson won in a canter.

I had a little better luck that year at Wimbledon. Fraser was beaten in one of the semifinals by Bobby Wilson of England, and I managed to produce all my good shots at once to beat Chuck McKinley in the final. This time I got the tactical advantage I could not get with Fraser by moving in and clubbing McKinley's service. It upset his serving

Margaret Smith returning a forehand drive (Mirror Newspapers Limited, Sydney)

rhythm, and he slowed it down to get more accuracy, and I just stepped in closer and closer and whacked the ball harder. Back in Australia Charlie Hollis listened to the matches on the radio, and crowed with delight. "I knew he'd be right as soon as I saw he wasn't going to play in that darn fool Mixed Doubles," Charlie said, pocketing the bets he had won on me. McKinley, in the final, was a little edgy at the start, and this gave me a chance to get over my slow start. Luck was with me, and after fifty-five minutes of it I mishit one off the wood which caught Chuck completely off-balance and won me the title 6–3, 6–1, 6–4. At last I had my hands on the Cup at my third final.

After my win over McKinley the British newspapers began to call me the "Rocket." Their descriptions will be good to read when I'm ready for the wheelchair. "The Australian redhead licked towards the net like a bushfire, decapitating McKinley's returns with backhand volleys rather like a man on a country stroll slashing off poppyheads with his walking stick," said the *Daily Mirror*. "Laver, the fourth left-hander and the eighth Aussie to win the title, returned service with such nonchalant power, hit such bristling drives, as nobody but a Hoad has been able to do in recent Wimbledons," the *Daily Express* said.

On my way home in 1961 we stopped off in Los Angeles for the Pacific Southwest Tournament, the last in the five months of weekly tournaments since we had left Australia. In Los Angeles I came home from a restaurant one night, and Roy Emerson came to my room and told me Frank Gorman was dead. Frank had been killed when a car he was driving crashed into a bridge. I just could not believe it. For days I went round in a daze trying to tell myself I must get used to what had happened. I still cannot believe it.

14. The Top Level

When you read about the big money the top professional tennis players earn you cannot help feeling envious. Not if you are practical. The figures are amazing. But unless you happen to be a competitor you will probably not understand that there is much more than money involved in giving up amateur tennis.

Ever since I can remember I have wanted to be the No. 1 tennis player in the world. I have had to take a lot of lickings before I got my big left arm around the real trophies, and I have tried to learn from these defeats. I am perfectly willing to take more lickings if they will make me a better player. I still have not lost sight of the fact that I want to be the best there is.

I am a competitor. Most days of my life I go out on a tennis court—temperamental weaknesses and all—and compete. For me there is nothing like it. This is a great way to live. You do not know how lucky I was when I decided to make competitive tennis my life.

Today, once you get near the top in amateur tennis, you cannot help but think of turning pro and whether it is worth it. First of all you think about the security the money will bring. Then because you have worked tremendously hard on your game and feel that you have reached the stage when nobody in amateur tennis can hurt you, a thought stirs around in your mind. How would your game stand up against the best pros?

I reached my fourth successive Wimbledon final in 1962, and was lucky enough to catch Marty Mulligan on an off day in the third leg of my Grand Slam. After the match I sat down, and talked about turning professional with Tony Trabert and Frank Sedgman. The year before, when I had beaten Chuck McKinley and won my first Wimbledon, Jack Kramer had offered me a guarantee of $35,000 to turn pro.

Now Trabert and Sedgman offered me double that for two years' play. I told them I did not want to make any decision until after I had played the final leg in the Slam, the United States Nationals. At Forest Hills when I made the Slam I told them I still did not want to make up my mind until I had got home. In any case, I wanted to help Australia defend the Davis Cup. I did not do this in any calculated way. I was simply too occupied with my tennis at this point to want to think things out. In the long run, waiting turned out pretty well because Trabert and Sedgman raised their ante to $100,000 to make sure they got me.

In the year of my Grand Slam my game changed. I lost a lot of my erratic habits. Perhaps because I was growing up my sloppiness disappeared. I got a little tougher on my opponents, although I doubt if I became the real killer Hoppy wanted to see. I concentrated better than I had ever done. People said I talked more. My confidence was higher in everything I did, whether it was wearing a tuxedo or dancing at the Wimbledon Ball or making a speech. It was important to me, though, that I still should not gloat over anyone I had beaten, and I tried always to remember Charlie Hollis's advice to console a loser—"Too bad, you played well," or "You hit some great shots"—something to show I wasn't cocky about winning and knew all too well how losing felt.

Fred Stolle, the Australian player who has known me for years, told an American reporter, "Rod isn't in as much of a shell as he used to be. It might seem that way to people who don't know him, but with the other players he's a lot looser than he used to be. He's quiet, but he likes to have a good time like everybody else. He's a great tennis player, but I don't think there's another player who resents his success because Rod has never made a big deal out of himself."

I was pretty excited about winning the Slam—the year of the Big Left Arm, someone called it. I played better than I expected, and I had the breaks, especially in France. When I gambled on my opponents' doing certain things they did what I wanted. Neale Fraser was probably right when he said I had improved fifteen points a game since 1960. Not only had all my speculative shots shaken down into a controlled game, but I was picking out more weaknesses in the players I met.

High or low returns on either side no longer bothered me. On the backhand, I could hit flat, top spin, or sliced shots across court and down the line, or could check and play a top-spin lob or a drop shot. With my forehand I had pretty good control. At the net my reflexes were good, and my volleys were going where I aimed them. My serve and overheads were reliable and strong, although I probably still could get more power into my serve. I could scramble, but mostly I tried to get myself out of any trouble by attacking the ball.

In Los Angeles shortly after I won the American title to join Don Budge in the Grand Slam club, I told the pros I'd be with them if my parents agreed. I wanted to talk with Dunlop's, too, to see how my deal there would be affected. After all, there were no more goals for me to aim at in amateur tennis now I had won the Slam.

Charlie Hollis had started me off with the Queensland Junior title, then the Australian Junior, then the Australian Open Singles in a graduated scale of achievement. The only place where there were still some goals to achieve, some fellows to beat, was with Ken Rosewall, Lew Hoad, Barry MacKay, Earl Buchholz, Andres Gimeno, and the other pros. And I had been promised $100,000 to test my tennis against players like that.

That last year as an amateur I had a great time, but I did not make a fortune. The story about my making $35,000 a year from amateur tennis was rot; I doubt if I had made $5,000.

I went back to Rockhampton, and told my dad I had made up my mind that I wanted to switch to the pros. He did not try to stop me. I think he and my brothers knew how I felt. It had been a hard road, and this way I might be able to relax in a few years without any financial worries. I had not been home for more than a few days at a time since I left to go to Brisbane, more than five years ago. Now I could get a few weeks off to go fishing with Trevor and Bob and make some plans about the squash courts we wanted to build together. While I was home on that trip I spent quite a bit of time going around to see old friends I had not had a chance to talk with in years. I really wanted to find out how they had got on and to pick up the threads of my school days.

The day I got home to Rockhampton after winning the Slam, they had a parade through the streets to welcome me. I planted the first tree in a new park they were laying out. At the races, they had me put the sash on the winning horse. There was a special dinner for me.

I went round the Australian amateur tournaments for the last time not worrying too much about the matches. My mind was mainly on my first match as a pro, which had been arranged for a week after the Davis Cup Challenge Round against Mexico. I had to play Lew Hoad in my pro debut on a Saturday night and Ken Rosewall on the following Sunday afternoon. I was to play twice in each capital city in Australia and then swing to New Zealand and the United States.

The Mexicans, I knew, could be very tough in the Challenge Round. The heat in Brisbane would suit them, and they had players each of whom was capable of inspired tennis if you let him get on top. I wanted to leave amateur tennis a winner, and even more I wanted Australia to keep the Davis Cup. But Harry Hopman really had to belt me hard to get me right, I had so many things on my mind.

Hop let me stay at the Shepherd house until a few days before the Challenge Round. I had grown to love that house and Mrs. Shepherd's home cooking. Mr. Shepherd had laid down a court in his backyard. All I had to do was to amble downstairs from the room they always kept for me and have a hit with Jim Shepherd, who was about two years younger than I was. Now, as we practiced to get ready for the Mexicans, I realized how much I owed the Shepherds and what a lot they had done for me in taking me into their home.

Just before the Cup matches I moved into the Australian team's hotel in central Brisbane. I had not sat down with the pros yet to work out the final details of my contract, but I knew I would be in a better position for my pro debut if I won these last matches as an amateur. I was not really concentrating on Palafox and Osuna, though. Lew Hoad and my first match against him as a pro dominated my thoughts.

Of all the great players I had met, I knew that Hoad was the man who liked playing left-handers more than anyone else. His enormous wrist development enabled him to take the ball very early on the rise, and this partly nullified the left-hander's natural advantages. He had my spin, but he also had power I could never hope to gain. He was a player to be admired by everyone who has ever whacked a ball over a tennis net.

On the eve of the Challenge Round a Sydney newspaper ran a story claiming Australia would be cheating by allowing me to play against the Mexicans. The paper reasoned that it was well known I was about to join the pros. Therefore I should be considered a pro, and left out of the Australian team. The president of the Lawn Tennis Association of Australia, apparently well aware that I was not doing anything that Frank Sedgman, Ken Rosewall, Ken McGregor, Lew Hoad, Ashley Cooper, Rex Hartwig, Mal Anderson, and others had done before, answered that there was no intention of omitting me from the Challenge Round matches unless there was a specific complaint from the Mexican team. Pancho Contrera, captain of the Mexican team, said they had no intention of doing so.

This turned out to be the most exciting part of my amateur tennis farewell. The matches themselves were fairly dull. I did not play well, but the Mexicans had not had sufficient grass-court practice, and they were at a big disadvantage when all five matches had to be played in spikes because of wet, slippery courts.

My pro debut with Hoad in Sydney earned me more money in one night than my profits from a full year as an amateur. My share of the gate was around £A2,500 ($4,592) for the four hard sets we played. Lew had been training for weeks to get ready for the match, and he made me aware immediately that the big pros jealously defend their reputations. In fact, the whole pro group descends on a newcomer like eagles on the lamb's back on the ranches in central Queensland. I had my chances in that first match, and if I had taken them I could have won. But I missed them, and Lew went on to win 8–6 in the fourth set. I enjoyed that match more than any I had played in years, and I think the crowd of around ten thousand did, too, because next day all the papers said we had brought back the excitement tennis had lacked in recent years.

Lew and I played until after 11 P.M., and by the time I got to bed it was almost 3 A.M. I woke about noon, and at 2 P.M. I had to go out and play Ken Rosewall in the second leg of our Sydney program. It was tough all right. I was so stiff after the long match with Hoad I could not run properly. I had lifted myself to a high pitch for Hoad and simply could not lift myself again after the letdown of losing. Ken took less than an hour to beat me in three sets.

Lew beat me in eight straight games after that, and Ken did it in eleven out of thirteen. On the highest level of the game, it looked as though my tennis education was just beginning. The difference between pro and amateur tennis was so great it took me months to settle down. I felt the pressure on my reputation as the top amateur, the man who had equaled Don Budge's Grand Slam, and there was a psychological barrier to break through that the pros had created.

On some occasions the ease with which they beat me, the constant traveling, the hard matches night after night without a spell made me feel like quitting. Then I would think of all I could do with the money, and console myself with my record: two Australian titles; two Wimbledon wins in four successive finals; the Grand Slam year, in which I had also won the fifth major title, the Italian.

I made steady progress in my game, and here and there I put on a show that gave me real hopes that I would end up the world's best player as I had always planned. One night at Madison Square Garden I swept through Rosewall in thirty-nine minutes, the first six games in only thirteen minutes with the loss of only nine points. Rosewall led 3–2 in the second set, but then I was on him again to take out the match 6–0, 6–3.

"Laver's game has progressed remarkably since his first New York appearance as a pro," wrote Allison Danzig in *The New York Times.* "He was hitting with the confidence of a master and with a speed that was sensational. The rapidity of his whipping ground strokes, loaded with spin, brought roars from the gallery, as did his vengeful volleys and overhead smashes."

If it were possible to reproduce tennis like that night after night for months on end, then the game would not be the great challenge it is to me and to all who play it. Within a few nights I was back to missing volleys and to flubbing a smash here and there, and some of the sting I had at Madison Square Garden had left my service. But I was working very hard on it, for I figured that I was now only one or two places from the top spot in world tennis. In that first year as a pro, I earned $75,000, sometimes at the fantastic rate of $40 a minute. The methods that had taken me from a back-yard court in a Queensland country town to the Grand Slam and to matches that ensured financial security for life had been well and truly vindicated.